P9-BIP-096

GOD BEYOND RELIGION

GOD BEYOND RELIGION

Personal Journeyings from Religiosity to Spirituality

George Bockl

DeVorss & Company
Box 550, Marina del Rey, CA 90294–0550

© 1988 George Bockl
All rights reserved

ISBN: 0-87516-612-1
Library of Congress Card Catalog Number: 88-51337

Printed in the United States of America

Dedicated to the Television Ministry
THERE IS A WAY

CONTENTS

Spirituality Brings Us Closer to God than Does Religiosity

Our civilization is at a new crossroad—secular politics is eroding durable values, and resurgent fundamentalism is igniting new religious divisions. It's a combustible mix. The "religionization" of politics and society is a response to the perceived failure of secular government. Iran, Egypt, and Israel are prime examples.

Dogmatic, separative religions have had their evolutionary cycle. It's time we began freeing ourselves from their domination. Religiosity civilized the world, but it also bloodied the world's history. We should give it a thankful goodby and offer a cheerful hello to the spiritual wave of the future.

Just as there have been three main cultural waves of change —the agricultural age, the industrial age, and now the informational age—so our God-yearnings have evolved from heathenism, to formal religion, and now into the spiritual age.

 Why does spirituality bring us closer to God than religiosity? Because religious petitionings, elaborate ceremonies, showy fanaticism, claims of special covenants, and charismatic leaders get between God and man. They stir up intense feelings that lead to clashes between the sacredness of one religion and the holiness of another.

What raises man's spirituality above the din of religious dogma is the transcendent music of metaphysical truth.

In the nineteenth century, Ralph Waldo Emerson and Abraham Lincoln heard this metaphysical truth and embraced its universal spirituality in preference to the prevailing practices. They were spiritual men in the highest religious sense of the word. In our own time, J. Krishnamurti, a spiritual revolutionary who has melded the spiritual wisdom of the East and West; Alexander Solzhenitsyn, who came out of Russia's atheism; and Ernest Holmes, who illumined the spiritual law that undergirds all religions—all have proclaimed that what the world needs is a spiritual renaissance that's more vital than today's mainstream pabulum religions.

Religiosity leads to an outer God. Spirituality penetrates to the God within us. That's why God is closer to us when we long for Him* in the privacy of our "closets" than in outer ceremonial tradition.

Are not unifying spiritual truths more believable than what comes out of the mouths of the charismatic evangelists who mesmerize their followers with fire-and-brimstone morality, and then themselves pursue the lowest kind of immorality?

Nor, in letting go of our religiosity, dare we fall into the trap of humanism. If we restrict ourselves to the intellect without an outlet to God, the mind turns on itself and normalizes all sorts of abnormalities.

What good is it to use our vaunted human reason to blame religions for using people as puppets, when we condemn ourselves to breathing the thin air of mortality instead of the spiritual oxygen of immortality?

Not for a moment should we harbor the thought that we

---

*References to God as He or Him are merely a convention adopted for the sake of simplicity in wording; they do not imply that God is more masculine than feminine or, for that matter, that there is any gender in God.

cannot make a difference in ushering in the new spiritual revolution. It's more exciting to be on the tip of spiritual evolution, even in the midst of discordant change, than to remain in a comfortable religious groove.

By replacing religiosity with spirituality, we shall remove walls between religions and build bridges between people.

One final note: I've chosen the anecdotal format to contrast spirituality with religiosity in the hope that these true but somewhat fictionalized personal stories will make for livelier, more realistic reading.

GOD BEYOND RELIGION

PART I

The Cosmic Connection

To conjecture idealism is easy; to live it is difficult. But without groping for plausible assumptions, there would be little civilizing progress. The most noble conjecture we can make is that somehow, some way, we are linked to a universal intelligence. This yearning to link up with it is the history of mankind's spiritual evolution.

Spiritual imagination, tempered by prudence, is the gateway to the unknown.

If we dream, let it be a noble dream, one that links us to a universal organism—a vast and mighty one without bounds. Only by dreaming do we awaken our awareness that we are part of this universal life-consciousness.

CHAPTER 1

Gropings

Deep in the heart of man is a longing to live for something great. The yearning is linked to a Cosmic Intelligence, and the line of communication is always open. That's why a scoundrel, no matter how fragile his connection with the divine, can eventually become a saint.

But because the connection is invisible, it's difficult to make it believable. The scientific revolution has conditioned us to believe only in what we see, and that makes the unmarked path from the lower to our higher human nature more difficult to tread.

We began our civilizing Godward journey some 5000 years ago with fetishes, sacrifices, and mythology. We refined it with dogma, proselytized it with ''holy'' wars, and merchandized it with missionaries. Millions died because the leaders couldn't agree on how to transmute our religious longings into a brotherhood and sisterhood of humanity.

After centuries of violence, the major religions have solidified their gains, but the twentieth century has threatened them from two diametrically opposed directions: the reawakening of fundamentalism and the growth of atheism. Iran is the ominous example of the one, the Soviet Union of the other. Between these two extremes, there's a slackening of dogma, people are changing from tighter to looser religions, and the walls between them are being replaced by bridges.

The era of relying on holy leaders for an interpretation of God is slowly ending. Because it has led to so much divisiveness and bloodshed, people are seeing the logic of taking charge of their own spiritual development.

The battle between personal and organized religion is a vexed problem. The arguments for and against each are equally and validly divided.

The following confrontation—at a typical symposium—is a microcosm of what is taking place with many variations in the Western world.

Arrayed against a rabbi, a priest, and a minister, were three laypersons—a Jew, a Catholic, and a Protestant. The moderator was a smartly dressed young woman psychologist. Her lively, intelligent eyes roved over an audience of several hundred people.

The Jewish layperson, a suave-looking thirty-year-old, spoke first. He directed his remarks to the three clergymen, but particularly to the rabbi.

"Inspired reading material is now available to the masses. Formerly, it was only available to the classes," he began. "By the classes, I mean the learned clergy who told their followers what to believe and what not to believe. By reading and thinking beyond my religion, I've liberated myself from your dogmatisms. I find a greater challenge in discovering spiritual truth myself than having it served up by tradition and digested by literalism."

"Do-it-yourself religious thinking may be all right for the few, but not for the many," replied the rabbi, who was wearing a yarmulke. "Without codifying the Jewish concept of God, individual religious effort would soon dissipate into a spiritless void, and Judaism with it. We must be practical, realistic. Most people will not take time to think for themselves. There're only a few like you. Our concern is for the many. They need our guidance, and we're not about to abdicate our duty to the millions of Jews for a few isolated ones like you.''

''But if the few see something more vital than what is being prescribed for the many,'' the Jewish layman rebutted, ''shouldn't we explore it, rather than keep ourselves bottled up in Talmudic lore?''

''Who says it's more vital? It's only your opinion against thirty-five hundred years of tradition,'' the rabbi shot back.

After several heated exchanges, the moderator called on the Catholic layperson, an immaculately dressed young woman.

''Although we come from different religious backgrounds,'' she said, turning to the Jewish speaker who preceded her, ''I have more in common with you than with my priest. Catholic fundamentalism has reached the end of a religious evolutionary cycle. We can no longer let its well-intentioned leaders do the thinking for us. New inspirational ideas are clamoring for our attention.''

The Roman-collared priest on the dais immediately moved in on the discussion.

''With apologies to the rabbi with whom I have more in common than with my Catholic rebel, I want to emphasize a very important point. Judaism's one-God concept would have remained a mere local discovery had it not been for us, who took it to the far corners of the earth. We turned heathens into God-loving people. We changed the course of history. After two thousand years of organizing and protecting our flock, we'd be derelict if we let our members wander aimlessly without our accumulated Catholic wisdom. If we did, there'd be a wholesale return to the heathenism from which we sprang.''

''Do I look like a heathen to you?'' the Catholic layperson asked. ''Without Catholic guidance, I feel closer to God than when I let the Pope do my thinking.''

"You may not look like a heathen, but without Catholic discipline, your children and your children's children would eventually be sucked into a spiritless void. I agree with the rabbi. The do-it-yourself, self-proclaimed experts will not improve on the religious wisdom of the ages."

The moderator stopped the verbal fireworks and called on the Protestant layman, a hippie-yuppie hybrid whose long hair contrasted with his striped gray suit.

"First," he began, "let me assure everybody in the audience that my two lay colleagues are not a couple of loose, freethinkers. On the contrary, they, like myself, are trying to practice a religion that requires more discipline than respectable church attendance. We're not satisfied with reaching for the Unknown through hurried hymns and holy sermons. We want more. We want to experience God with all the pluralistic insights we can glean, from whatever source, and fashion them into a spiritual discipline that requires more than mere adherence to rite and rote. We want to raise the moral quality of our lives, not because some church authority tells us to do it, but because we're convinced of it ourselves."

"Let's hear now," said the moderator politely, "what the Protestant minister has to say about this young heretic."

The minister, not much older than his Protestant counterpart, rose from his seat and walked to the lectern.

"The three rebels," he began, "have overlooked an important fact. Religions haven't stultified, they've been constantly reforming, revising, and loosening their dogmas. The Jews discovered, the Catholics merchandized, and the Protestants have refined the concept of God. To give up what we've learned for a do-it-yourself kind of religion would be like wiping out all we've learned about electricity and starting all over again. The falling away from organized religion has brought cynicism, despair, drugs, and a proliferation of cults in search of quick answers. I agree that religions need improvising, but let's do it within the time-tested truths, not by loners or guru followers. A coal at the edge of a burning pile cools quickly. Within the pile each receives heat from the other. On the outside, it becomes just an unused piece of cold carbon."

"Do you feel the cold outside the burning pile," the moderator asked the Protestant layman, "or have you found a new way to remain warm outside the heap?"

The ex-Protestant rose slowly. The minister struck a cogent blow against individual religion. The audience waited eagerly for the reply.

"What if the burning pile accomplished nothing more than burning itself out into slag? Or worse, if the fire jumped and burned other piles into slag—you know what I mean: proselytizing."

The audience seemed to like the quick retort. The Protestant layman raced on.

"I'm not for gurus or cults, nor for fooling around with shallow substitutes. What my colleagues and I are proposing, is letting the full-grown religions die gracefully. Their cycle is over—even as cycles of civilizations are born, grow old, and die. New buds are forming everywhere to unite the world into what Teilhard de Chardin calls a new global theosphere—a common spirituality. New spiritual shoots are growing, inspiring new ideas about God. For instance, no longer is sin looked upon by liberated people like us with the old biblical fire and brimstone, but as foolish mistakes that gum up our lives. I could cite other examples."

The moderator got up from her chair. "This is a good note on which to end the panelists' discussion. Now, ladies and gentlemen, you can ask questions from the floor."

A well-groomed, middle-aged woman, a typical parishioner of the kind you would expect to find in a fashionable Episcopalian church, walked to the microphone, and in a deliberate, articulate voice put this question to each of the three laypersons:

"Despite religious divisiveness, you will have to admit there is discipline within each denomination, especially where it is needed: among the uneducated. What makes you think that, by loosening these organizational bonds into unorganized personal religion, it will not degenerate into a babel of subjective chaos? Dare we gamble our mature stability for the upheavals of the Moonies, Hare Krishnas, and the do-it-yourself wanderers that are getting people into drugs, free love, and suicide? Dare we tinker with something that has worked, that has civilized the world?"

The Jewish layperson was first to respond.

"Why not gamble with the new? The situation we've inherited has created centuries of prejudice and violence. At the tip of change there's always discordance. We must risk the discordance—the gurus, the cults, the aimless wanderings. But they'll disappear, and the restless searchers will eventually find their answers in self-disciplined spirituality."

The Catholic layperson gave a short answer.

"We have too many religious leaners, and not enough spiritual lifters. By lifting, I mean more personal effort to reach for God than leaning on church attendance."

The Protestant layperson was just as succinct.

"Whether we like it or not, the flow from organized to personal religion is gaining momentum. Solzhenitsyn's hope for a global spiritual renaissance and Teilhard de Chardin's forecast of a spiritual mutation are harbingers of the change we're talking about."

The forum we've been listening in on is only a paraphrase of the collision between religiosity and spirituality, which has been documented by, among others, Charles S. Braden in his *Spirits in Rebellion*—a researched account of the new thought about religion that is spreading in Western countries.

Why is the metaphysical so real to some and an idle abstraction to others? Why is karma regarded as a fact of life in the East and a curiosity in the West?

What is the rationale for viewing life as a constant becoming, a never-ending climbing, where the journey becomes the destiny, in contrast to stopping in heaven and living in perfection forever?

Why do some seek to open their cosmic connection, while others clog it up with materialism, hedonism, and atheism?

Trying to answer these and other questions led me from the noise of real estate wheeling and dealing to a quiet vision, flashing with grandeur.

PART II

Why People Change from Closed Religions to Open-Ended Spirituality

The transition from parochialism to universalism is accelerating. Liberal parishioners are leaving tightly organized religions for looser ones.

The elderly are still traveling Godward baggaged with rules and ceremonials, but the young are clearing away the doctrinal debris for a more open-ended channel to God.

The following stories are a microcosm of the religious transformations that are taking place.

CHAPTER 2

Esther's Battle—from Judaism to Theosophy

Esther led a comfortable, middle-class life in a Jewish orthodox home until she enrolled in a college and took a course in comparative religion. She was introduced to Theosophy—a synthesis of Eastern and Western spiritual wisdom, which underscores the essential unity of all religions.

Esther became enamored of this new knowledge and knew that her parents would be against her delving into it.

"What kind of *mishugayes* are you getting yourself into?" her mother chided when Esther stopped going to synagogue with her family on Friday nights.

"It's not a *mishugayes*, mother. I feel more at peace with the theosophical God than the vague one you've got in your religion."

Her mother looked at her with a mixture of anger and disbelief.

"What do you mean—'your' religion?" she snapped. "Remember, as long as you're a member of this family, *our* religion is *your* religion. And don't you forget it. The Jewish God has been with us for 5000 years, and you're not going to throw Him away for some fad like Theofoshy, or whatever you call it. It's a nothing compared to the wisdom of Judaism!"

"I'm not against Judaism, mother. I just want a more plausible meaning of God than the primitive one of Abraham,

13

Isaac, and Jacob. There's been a lot of new thinking since the Jews discovered God. I want to keep abreast. That's not irreligious; it's being *more* religious.''

''Look, I see you're pretty deep in whatever you're in, so before you get over your head, let's discuss it with your father and brothers. They'll pound some sense into you.''

Esther's mother was smart enough to know that she was no match for her college-educated daughter. She needed the help of her more worldly husband and three college-educated sons.

On a Sunday afternoon, Esther's family gathered in the living room to discuss their problem. Her three brothers and their wives and children were there. Esther hoped for a discussion, not a confrontation. She wanted to retain the warmth of her family.

Abraham, Esther's father, spoke first.

''I want you to look around this room, Esther. It's a wonderful family, isn't it? That's Judaism. And when Jews help other Jews as we do all over the world, that's an extension of the Jewish family. It took a lot of wisdom, and many centuries of persecution, to develop this precious Jewishness. And you want to cut yourself off from this wonderful heritage? Give it up for something you've read—that's here today and gone tomorrow?''

Esther's mother was proud of her husband. He praised his Judaism so much better than she could. Esther, too, was impressed, but arguments quickly lined up to counter him.

''I have no quarrel with what you're saying, father. Judaism has a great deal of wisdom, but so have Christianity, Buddhism, and Hinduism. Can you blame me for wanting a wisdom that combines the wisdom of *all* religions? I'm not blaming you for limiting your God to Judaism, but please don't blame me for wanting a God who is unlimited, more believable.''

Her father's face reddened.

"Judaism does not limit me. There's enough wisdom in Judaism to spend a lifetime and only get a glimpse of it. You're mimicking the prattlings of false prophets, you're blaspheming a deeply rooted religious faith."

"That's where you're wrong, father. Theosophy not only deepens my faith in God, it explains God, makes Him more vibrant and believable. Would you care to hear how I came to that conclusion?"

"Let her, Dad," urged Harry, the eldest brother. "Let's hear what she has to say."

Esther looked around the room to get her entire family's attention.

"God, pictured as a white-bearded man somewhere in the sky who sees all and knows all, punishes and rewards, is an antiquated concept which has served its purpose. Today, thinking people no longer believe in an anthropomorphic God, that the world was created in six days, in the literal translation of the Bible. Theosophy does not discard God; on the contrary, it revitalizes Him with the spiritual wisdom of the East and West into a Universal Intelligence. But before you get any idea that this concept removes the personal I-Thou relationship, let me quickly add, it does not."

"How?" Harry asked.

"The explanation may sound new and strange to you, but please hear me out. Theosophy is really not a religion. It's a body of spiritual truths that form the basis of all religions, and which cannot be claimed as the exclusive possession of any. It's studied, not worshipped, by men and women in over seventy countries. Its main goal is to make God central in their lives through a recognition of three important cosmic laws: evolution, karma, and reincarnation."

"You're wasting your time," her father cut in. "All your fancy explanations make God less, not more, believable. Your blabberings don't make sense."

"Let her finish," the eldest son urged again.

"Thanks, Harry." Esther cast an appreciative glance in his direction.

"Be patient. Please hear me out. Evolution is a fact, and karma and reincarnation are its logical consequences. Karma is a universal law of cause and effect which Ralph Waldo Emerson introduced us to 150 years ago. If we lead a low life, we'll get low returns. If we lead a good life, we'll get high returns. The third cosmic law is reincarnation. Just as matter in our bodies is not lost when we die, but merely changes into another form, so individualized consciousness at death is not lost but changes into another existence on what's called the astral plane. Then it dies and moves to the mental plane, and finally it returns to a physical body for more spiritual experience."

"How do all these mental gymnastics get you closer to God?" the youngest brother asked.

"Let me finish, Ben, then you'll see. Reincarnation answers the puzzling question why bad guys seem to get good breaks and good guys, bad ones. The law of karma does not work out its cause and effect in only one lifetime. Without the law of reincarnation, there would be no justice in having a wonderful young man die at twenty, and a scoundrel live to the ripe old age of eighty. The law of karma makes you pay for your mistakes, if not in the present lifetime, then in the next. And the karmic rewards may likewise be delayed until another incarnation. If death is thus put in its rightful place, as a recurring incident in an endless life, then living opens the gateway to a fuller and more radiant existence. As you can see, Theosophy doesn't rely on a vague heaven but on a much more scientific explanation of God's life-governing laws. That's what makes Him more believable. I'm afraid I've talked too long. I'd rather you ask questions if there's anything that puzzles you."

"What puzzles me," her father exploded, "is why an intelligent Jewish girl like you should get mixed up with something as un-Jewish as all this malarkey. Unless you stop tinkering with this crazy mishmash, you're not going to be welcome in this house. If you want to be part of us, you'll have to choose between your *mishugayes* and the warmth of your family in this living room.''

''Why can't I remain part of the family, each giving freedom to the other?''

''Because,'' her mother cut in, ''there can't be togetherness when we're so far apart.''

''Esther,'' Harry added, ''we've listened patiently to your explanations. We're not in the least interested. I can give you a dozen reasons, but if you still insist on being part of your new thing, you cannot be part of us—that's final.''

''Then I choose my thing, and let me point out the difference between your attitude and mine. I don't blame you for remaining in your comfortable religion, but you condemn me for trying to find a common spiritual ground so that Arabs and Jews can stop hating each other. Theosophy is not a cult like the Moonies or Hare Krishnas. It's the rising up of a new breed of people to form a universal spiritual nucleus without distinction of race, creed, sex, or color.''

She had caught an eloquent theosophical wave and ridden it to the crest.

''That's enough,'' Abraham snapped. ''You know where we stand.''

''Yes, I know. You're cutting *me* off, but Theosophy teaches me not to cut *you* off. You're going to be my family even though our religious views are centuries apart. It should also give you some idea how each of us practices our religion.''

I got this story from Esther at her vegetarian restaurant.

''Old religions are holding on,'' she told me after lunch one day, ''but their incrustations are cracking under the impact of questing minds. The literal truth of the Bible is waning, and self-searching is gaining.''

''That's lofty rhyme,'' I complimented. ''I wonder if

there's danger in your becoming more intellectual than spiritual, as your family feared.''

She smiled.

''Yes, there's always that danger. Intellect sometimes overpowers faith. But without reason, faith becomes blind.''

''Let's not get too serious. Are you happy? Any regrets?''

''Yes, I'm happy. Regrets? Some . . . I miss the warmth of my family. Even though I understand why they're shunning me, and I forgive them, it still hurts. And I feel badly because I know it hurts them too. But that's spiritual evolution at work. There's bound to be turbulence when the old gives way to the new. I lost familial love, but I found a wider window on eternity.''

My encounter with Esther led me to a lifelong study of Theosophy. Its spiritual wisdom inspired a grander and more encompassing view of God and the universe. It distilled the differences between spirituality and religiosity more comprehensively than any body of views I had so far come across. It helped me to formulate a master plan for living.

Theosophy does not profess a common belief, but a common search for Truth. It regards Truth as a prize to be striven for, not as a dogma to be imposed by authority. One of its attractions for me was that the noble truths that form the basis of all religions should not be claimed as the exclusive possession of any.

Theosophy puts death in its rightful place—as a recurring incident in an endless life, opening the gateway to a fuller and more radiant existence. While Theosophy does not, and cannot, prove this point, its literature argues convincingly of its plausibility.

From out of all these considerations there emerged a teaching whose attractions for Esther became real for me too.

CHAPTER 3

How the Baha'i Faith
Lit Up Two Orthodox Lives

They were 3000 miles apart, Maya in Los Angeles and Phil in New York, wallowing in the miseries of their despairing lives. Maya, 27, had tried to find happiness as an extra in Hollywood; and Phil, 40, was winding up an unhappy marriage in the Bronx. Both had nothing big to live for except adjusting to the emptiness of their lives.

I met them almost 30 years ago in Milwaukee when, wearied by their pasts, they came to the Middle West to reconstruct their lives.

I was building the first modern office building in the city and had been floundering in the myriad details of satisfying the precise tenant demands of doctors, lawyers, and insurance executives, when Phil walked into my office and asked for a job. I looked up from my desk and heaved a sigh.

"If you were a trained leasing expert, maybe. . . ."

"I'm a lawyer, and I catch on quickly," he cut in. "I can relieve you of your burden, and mine."

"What do you mean, yours?"

In the next half-hour he described his adult life. He was reared by middle-class orthodox Jewish parents. After graduating from law school, he looked forward to a happy life married to

19

a psychology major. But instead of fusing their intellects, they clashed, each cutting up the other until their hostilities exploded into a divorce. It embittered Phil's life. When psychiatry didn't help, he tried roaming across the face of Europe to calm his mental turmoil but found no relief.

"I'm still full of hostility," Phil admitted; "but I've also got lots of ability. Work will help me get rid of my poison, and you'll be getting help at a bargain. I don't care how much you pay. Just let me work for you."

I hired him.

It was an excellent decision, for him and for me. Not only did he do a masterful job of satisfying tenant demands, but within a short time I made him president of my leasing department.

Phil remained his clever, cutting self, while we made giant commercial strides together. His sharp mind matched his sharp tongue.

"Are you aware, Phil," I asked one morning, "that you're *against* everything—and most vehemently against your Jewish religion? Why?"

"I have good reason."

"Why your religion?"

"Because it's done nothing for me. I'm up to *here* with Jewish platitudes. Work has saved me from going under, not religion."

"Have you given it a chance?"

"No use. I'm smarter than the rabbis. What can they teach me that I haven't read in the Bible?"

"Has psychiatry taught you more?"

"Psychiatry isn't worth a damn either. In fact, I haven't found anyone I couldn't outsmart—including you, if you want to know," he said with a smirk.

"Is being smart enough?"

"It's good enough for me."

Things began to change when Phil met Maya. In his rest-lessness, he walked into a meeting one evening where a group of people were listening to Maya explain the wisdom of the Baha'i Faith. Her sincerity and elegant dignity attracted him more than what she was saying. What he saw was an attractive young woman who was aflame with an ideal that had burned out what was left of her Catholicism and all the vestiges of her former Hollywood culture.

One day Phil introduced me to Maya. After a few pleasantries, I asked, "Maya, you're changing Phil for the better. Is it the Baha'i faith or you?"

She looked at Phil for permission to expound her newly found commitment.

"Go ahead, Maya," he encouraged; "give him the full treatment." There was more affection in Phil's face than I had ever seen before.

"I was restless," she began. "More than restless, I was desperate. I felt myself slipping into the messy lives of my Hollywood friends. I felt an emptiness amidst their noisy excitement. I came back to the Midwest, where I was born, reaching for a straw. A friend invited me to a Baha'i talk. Instead of a straw, I found a rock."

"What did the speaker say that got you on that rock?"

"A very simple thing. Seeking God with friends through informal discussions, instead of going to Catholic mass, singing hymns, and hearing the same old doctrines over and over again."

"What, specifically, makes Baha'i different from other faiths?"

"Progressive revelation. Let me explain. God communicates with mankind from time to time through prophets who provide new spiritual teachings to advance man's development. Each succeeding prophet confirms the validity of the previous ones. Bahaullah is the prophet for our time, after Abraham, Krishna, Moses, Buddha, Christ, and Muhammad."

"How structured is Bahaism?"

"There're no professional clergy. No one earns a living from it. The faith is spread and administered by local spiritual assemblies, who meet at national assemblies once a year, and at an international assembly in Haifa, Israel, every five years, where they elect nine members to administer the Baha'i Faith throughout the world."

"Isn't this like the Sanhedrin of the Hebrews and the Vatican of the Catholics today?"

"There's a similarity, but Bahaullah's spiritual message is entirely different. It deals with the problems of our present civilization."

"Like what?"

"Like the *oneness of religion*—that religion should not be fragmentized into dogmas that divide people."

"You're so fluent. What's the source of your eloquence?"

"When you're on fire, you talk from the heart. That's more eloquent than the mind."

"Go on," I said. "This is interesting."

Phil smiled his approval.

"Let me point to Bahaullah's views that had not been enunciated by the previous prophets—individual search for truth, the equality of men and women, the harmony of science and religion, the elimination of extreme wealth and poverty, the need for world government, and the protection of cultural diversity. All these did not apply to the times of the previous prophets, but they do now."

"Is the Baha'i Faith making any headway?"

She was obviously pleased with the question.

"There are 132 national assemblies in 132 countries and approximately 110,000 localities where Baha'is reside. Approximately 1700 tribes and minority groups are represented in the faith, and Baha'i literature has been translated into 650 dialects and languages. This should give you an idea of the headway we're making to unite the diverse peoples of the world with the newest message from God."

A few days later Phil walked into my office.

"I'd like to get your advice, George. Maya wants to marry me. I'm holding off because I was hurt by my previous marriage. Do you think it could work? Could she crack a hard guy like me with her soft Baha'i Faith? She thinks she can convert me. I don't think so. And there lies the dilemma. Can a marriage divided, half Baha'i, half Jewish, stand up?"

"Your marriage will stand up provided you change your views to hers."

"But what happens if I put out her flame with my cold logic? I can be very persuasive, you know."

"I don't think you will. She'll melt your logic before you put out her flame. Go ahead, marry her."

Phil hadn't entirely unharnessed himself from his Jewishness. He wanted a Jewish marriage by a rabbi. Maya was content with an informal ceremony attended by a few Baha'i friends. The problem was solved when Phil couldn't find a rabbi to marry them. That dried up what little Jewishness he still possessed and subsequently pushed him closer to Maya's Bahaism.

The rest is commercial and spiritual history. Phil left me to form his own firm and became a millionaire. He's retired now. Maya has broken through his cold logic, and converted him into a passionate Baha'i. He devotes a great deal of his time proclaiming Bahaullah's message in many parts of the country. Recently I received a letter from him:

Dear George,

I'm devoting most of my time to furthering Progressive Revelation, the principle that God communicates with mankind through periodic appearances of prophets to meet the current spiritual needs of people.

I found it easy to move from Judaism to the teachings of Bahaullah. The spiritual wisdom I learned as a Jew is still with me. I gave up only the synagogues and the rabbis. I now fully accept the teachings of Christ, but not the rite and rote that grew out of his teachings. I accept the revelations of the previous prophets, but not the stultifying rules built around them. For me, Bahaism is both the oldest and the newest religion, as old as the first prophet, and as new as Bahaullah.

Cordially yours,

Phil

For Maya and Phil, Progressive Revelation was the persuasive principle that moved them from their old religious moorings to the new. The same experience would repeat itself in the lives of others I came to know. Each followed his or her drummer, and in each case the change from tighter to looser religions was accompanied by less dogmatism and more open-ended thoughtfulness.

Diversity was still there, but their views were moving toward a more unifying spirituality.

CHAPTER 4

Why a Methodist Minister Became a Buddhist Monk

I find meeting unusual people in unusual places more interesting than sightseeing or looking for offbeat restaurants. Within two days after arriving in Hawaii, I had arranged a meeting with an unusual man.

I met Wesley in his office adjoining an ornate Buddhist temple. His clipped accent was British to the core, but his robe and mindset were those of a Buddhist monk.

While on a trip to the Far East, Wesley had become so enamored of the Buddha's wisdom that he gave up his Methodist ministry to devote his remaining years to a new clerical role. He chose Hawaii because it was at the crossroads of East and West, the clashpoint of his former and his new religion.

After a few conversational preliminaries, I asked the question uppermost on my mind.

"I can understand a Christian changing from one denomination to another—but from Christianity to Buddhism? Why?"

"Because Christianity is a closed system, while Buddhism is open-ended. It was a quantum jump—not easy. But after studying Buddhism for several years, I found its wisdom so grippingly relevant, that I couldn't in good conscience continue preaching Christianity."

"Explain the difference between a closed and an open system."

"Christian belief is circumscribed by doctrine. Buddhism has no frontiers, and it's not in opposition to any religion."

"Please be more specific."

"Buddhism makes no claim to the possession of the final truth. Eventually such 'truth' dies through repetition. It's not creative, it doesn't evolve."

"How come you didn't know this before you met Buddhism?"

"I was too busy with Christianity to inform myself about other faiths. But when I met Buddhism while on a vacation trip to the Far East, I was transformed by its wisdom, and I'm here to transform others because it has so much to offer to the West. But frankly, it's an uphill battle. Not many are listening."

"Why not?"

"Because Christians cling to tradition."

"But so does Buddhism, with its temples, monasteries, and statues."

"Yes, but not to the extent that Christianity does."

"So far, you've told me how it's different. How is it wiser?"

"It's wiser because Buddhism doesn't take sides. Its universality speaks to all people everywhere who are concerned with achieving a meaningful life. It doesn't elevate a god over man, because when the ultimate is elevated over the immediate, then life becomes chained to an abstraction."

"Explain that, please."

"The religions of the West are dualistic. They elevate the ideal over the prosaic, heaven over earth. But life will not submit for long to such a division. The devalued fragments periodically reassert themselves into materialism, atheism, and individualism. The wisdom of Buddhism is that truth must never be sought on the plane of opposites, where one tries in vain to subdue one half of himself by the other, the natural by the supernatural. The path of transcendence, which has been mistakenly chosen by most religions, is an idolatrous substitute for authentic religion.''

''But your duality indictment is contrary to the very core of all the world's religions.''

''Yes, I know, and the Muslims and Christians are still suffering from these dualities. Muslims go into battle to martyr themselves for the idolatrous abstraction of ending up in heaven. And the Christians have done it during the Inquisition. For Buddhists, giving one's life in opposition to another's belief is sheer absurdity. For us, life is wholeness, responding to wholeness, out of which flows a love of unconditioned union with all that is. Now perhaps you have some idea why I was won over.''

''So far it all sounds very secular. What do you teach people?''

''How to attain an ideal state of intellectual and ethical perfection by purely human means. The Buddha, without claiming divinity, was the epitome of human perfection. No world teacher was as godless as the Buddha, yet few more Godlike. That should give you a pretty good idea of how different Buddhism is from other religions.''

''How did the Buddha change hundreds of millions without using transcendent means?''

''By dramatizing human truths so that people could become perfected human beings.''

''What truths?''

''The Four Noble Truths—the heart of the Buddha's teaching. The Noble Truths of the existence of suffering, the origin of suffering, the extinction of suffering, and the path leading to the extinction of suffering. Those who develop an understanding of these four truths can win the supreme enlightenment which frees man from the miseries of the world. I teach these truths in this temple.''

''Let's take the first—the existence of suffering. What's so new about it? Don't we all know it?''

''Yes, but do we really understand its origin? Most are not

aware that it starts with thoughtless cravings, possession cravings, power cravings, sensual cravings. That's how suffering takes root—pursuit of pleasurable feelings. Inevitably they end in the opposite—suffering.''

''All right, you've explained the cause of suffering. But how do we end it?''

''That's more crucial, more important. It requires two major decisions. First, avoid attachments however pleasurable, and second, follow the Buddha's Noble Eightfold Path— standards of thought and conduct that lead away from the temporary and pleasurable to the durable and blissful.''

''Describe a person who understands the Four Noble Truths and follows the Noble Eightfold Path.''

''Such a one is no longer afflicted with the tension between desires and duties which burden Western man. He's not torn with the dualism of wishing to serve God while being tempted by the Devil, of pledging allegiance to heaven, yet not being able to withstand the lure of earthly pleasures—you know, St. Paul's dualism of the flesh warring against the mind. A mind in pieces cannot be a mind at peace. A Buddhist following the Eightfold Path is at peace because there are no warring opposites as in other religions. He is graced with simplicity and dignity. He is distinguishable from others by the attractiveness of his manners and serene composure. His wisdom lies in his belief that no word of God prescribed by any clergy can express his earthly individuality unless God is none other than his own true self.''

''You've raised a lot of questions, and answers with which I don't agree; but for now, tell me more about the Eightfold Path.''

''I'll just give you the skeleton. Only when it's fleshed out with explanations, anecdotes, parables, and examples can it change an ordinary person into one with extraordinary qualities. The eight character builders are: right understanding, right mindedness, right speech, right action, right living, right

effort, right attentiveness, and right concentration. Very simple, but implementing them is a lifelong challenge. They lead
to human perfection.''

''What you've been saying so far merely refines and institu-
tionalizes secular humanism. You've given up the concept of
God for the perfection of man. I don't think you've made a
good trade. Your human god does not stack up to a transcendent God. And by the way, what about the statues, the ornate
temple, and the saffron robe you're wearing? Aren't these
trappings similar to those of a closed religious system?''

''It's an insignificant similarity. The essence of our beliefs,
however, is totally different.''

''Let's end on at least one point of agreement. We see eye to
eye on the need to loosen the dogmas of old religions. We differ, however, on the means. I believe in changing from a religious God to a spiritual God, you from a Christian God to a
human god.''

I was informed, but not transformed.

I prided myself on having an open mind, but not so open as
to let go of a belief in a transcending Intelligence that is the
living source of my life.

CHAPTER 5

Why a Private Detective Changed from Catholicism to Spiritual Science

Matt was a good Irish Catholic until he became disturbed by the different views of God in his courses on comparative religion at Ohio University. When he asked his priest about those conflicting ideas, he was told, "Go home and pray."

"I need more than prayers," Matt insisted. "I need explanations."

"You'll find them in prayer," the priest repeated.

Matt left the priest's study and eventually the Catholic Church. He became an atheist, and after wandering aimlessly for a few years, took a job as a private detective.

That was thirty years ago. Now, as I sat across Matt's desk in his office adjoining his Religious Science Church in a prominent California city, I looked at the joyous 55-year-old man and wondered.

"You were a private eye," I said, "and now you're the minister of a church with a thousand members. That's quite a switch, and an accomplishment in a city known for its infatuation with celebrities, restaurants, and conspicuous consumption. Why are people flocking to hear your sermons?"

"No, not sermons, but explanations and demonstrations of how spiritual science changes lives."

"But your church is known as Religious Science. Why did you refer to it as spiritual science?"

30

"Because we began using 'Religious' Science years ago when the difference between religious and spiritual was not as precise as it is today. Some day we'll change it to *Spiritual Science.*"

"Now that you've cleared away an important point, may I ask why you've forsaken your Catholic God for a spiritual-science God? What's the difference?"

He smiled, his lively grey eyes warm with joy.

"The difference is the story of my life. Neither Catholicism nor atheism fulfilled me. For a while, only sleuthing and my liking for people kept me afloat."

"Then what happened?"

He didn't need much nudging.

"Thirty years ago, a friend of mine invited me to attend a Religious Science church service. What I heard was so radically different from my Catholic religion, and so believable, that I decided then and there to find out more about it. I did, and what I learned was so revolutionary that I decided to devote the rest of my life to it."

"What makes Religious Science, or shall we say Spiritual Science, so revolutionary and more believable than other religions?"

"It's a new ball game. The main objective of Religious Science is to take God from somewhere out *there*, and put Him right *here*," he said pointing to his heart. "Let me explain. Very simply, we believe that the Cosmos is fundamentally a Universal Energy with Intelligence, Purpose, and Order. Whether we call it God, Nature, or Spirit, it is the Power that runs our minds, bodies, and everything in the Universe. We can use this Power only to the extent that we understand it."

"How are you different from those who understand and use 'Bible Power'?"

"We do not deal with allegories, mythologies, or symbols. They confuse rather than clarify. We try to be more scientific. Just as there's a science of physics, so there's a science of mind. Just as we can depend on the law of gravity, so can we depend on the Law of Mind. When we think a thought into this Law of Mind, we can expect a matching result in the same way as we expect it with the law of gravity.''

''Wait a minute. Do you mean the mind reacts to thoughts as precisely as an object falls to earth?''

''Yes! It works with precision. But we get what we want only to the extent of our belief that what we put in the mind, it reproduces. That's our only limitation—the strength of our belief. The model we form in our mind attracts the Energy to produce it.''

''Very interesting, and impressively fluent for a private eye!''

''I owe it to Ernest Holmes and his book *The Science of Mind*, where most of my ideas come from.''

''Is it your Bible?''

''Not the way you mean it. Religious Science is not a parochial system. It grows continually as humankind evolves, drawing on frontiers of new knowledge.''

''What new knowledge have you discovered about God?''

''That God is not some vague, invisible, fathomless entity, but as real as the wisdom that operates our bodies, as tangible as our consciousness, as visible as the earth and the billions of stars in the Universe. That's our living, visible God from whom we draw our power to advance our evolution.''

''Can this Power be demonstrated, used in a practical way?''

''Yes, by using the Law of Mind. But let me repeat, should all the Wisdom of the Universe be poured over us, we could only use that which we understand. That's why we have to study it, understand it, believe it, before we can use it.''

''This is beginning to sound like Christian Science.''

''Yes, the basic principle is the same—our Law of Mind parallels their Divine Mind. However, we emphasize spiritual science, while they emphasize Christian Science. Ours is more universal. We've incorporated new strands of spiritual wisdom that reflect more than a half-century of new thinking since Mary Baker Eddy's discovery of Christian Science.''

''Does the healing part differ?''

"Yes. Christian Science maintains that matter is mortal mind's illusion. We believe that matter is part of reality, and so we do not discourage the use of medication when the patient desires it. Nor do we deny that some mental ills can be cured by psychiatry. The Law of Mind operates essentially the same as does Divine Mind, but we see and understand it as the certain operation of a very real and simple *law*, which Christian Science does not acknowledge as such. I also think that we use this law equally for preventing as well as healing diseases."

"How do you prevent diseases?"

"We emphasize joy. Not a foolish show of happiness, but a quiet joy that comes from our gratefulness for life. When we put this joyous energy into the pipeline of the Law of Mind, it dissolves anxiety, fear, and all the myriad anti-life thoughts that are prime causes for disease. When any disequilibrium slips through our joyous guard, relying on God's natural wisdom of the body puts it back in equilibrium. It's the most efficacious method to prevent the disturbance from developing. But it has to be backed up with an unswerving conviction. It has worked for me, and I've seen it work for others. Prevention is intertwined with joy, and joy with love. I'd like to end my long dissertation with one of Ernest Holmes' scientific quotations: 'Love points the way, and the Law of Mind makes the way possible.'"

"I know you have an appointment, but before I leave, please tell me what exactly is your work in the church?"

"I conduct two Sunday services a week, I counsel, and I teach introductory and practitioner courses as well as courses for prospective ministers."

"Are there other less structured religions like yours, using different names, that are spreading the same kind of universal spiritual gospel?"

"Yes, Unity School of Christianity, Divine Science, Theosophy, and small associations with various names that are breaking out of old religious molds. It all started with Phineas

Parkhurst Quimby, and the seed is now sprouting and spreading with accelerating speed. If you want to get an optimistic view of how fast we're moving away from the religious to the spiritual age, I suggest you read *The Aquarian Conspiracy*, by Marilyn Ferguson, and *Spirits in Rebellion*, by Charles Braden. Both show, in researched detail, how men and women are articulating the defects of antiquated fundamentalism. To bring it close to home, there's a daily television program that dramatizes our new spiritual thinking. It has a viewing audience of 1,250,000, and its name is "There Is a Way."

"Any other parting views?"

"I'm saddened by the tragedy that hundreds of millions of people are still struggling in the darkness of their rickety religions, or in barren atheism, when they can use spiritual science to lighten and gladden their lives. It's as if they had grand pianos in their minds, but were not using the Law of Mind to learn how to play them. The Law of Mind is like a universal computer with which we can plug in to information that's good for us and get a printout to match."

"You've given me a lot to think about. Anything more?"

"The line to God is always open. Every call we make scientically is an expression of joy, a healing treatment, because every time we dial, God responds to our needs on the other end of the line."

I attended several Sunday Religious Science services and saw how this former detective joyously lifted the thinking of retired industrialists, active businessmen, and—sprinkled among them—many youthful faces.

I was struck by an emerging mutational fact: religiosity was changing to spirituality. The audience was enthusiastically responding to new thinking—leaving passive tradition in order to actively explore a more vibrant concept of God.

CHAPTER 6

Why Douglas Changed from Episcopalianism to Christian Science

As in nature, there are ebbs and flows in people, and I've had my share of them. I was in one of those lows one Sunday morning about thirty years ago and decided to lift myself out of it by attending a Christian Science Church service. I had never been to one, but several of my friends extolled its uplifting power.

An usher met me at the door and courteously escorted me to a seat a few rows in front of a rostrum. I found myself in a large, well-lit, plain room that looked more like an auditorium than a church. Casually, I began to study some of the people in the audience. My impression of the some 300 well-dressed men and women was that they were mostly middle-class, and sprinkled among them I recognized a few of my business friends.

At eleven o'clock sharp, a man and a woman walked onto the rostrum from opposite side doors and sat down on two chairs behind a centrally situated lectern. After a man with a deep baritone voice sang a hymn and left the platform, the woman, who I later learned was the "Second Reader," read short passages from the Bible. The man, who was the "First

Reader,'' followed her with correlative passages from the Christian Science textbook, *Science and Health with Key to the Scriptures*, by Mary Baker Eddy, the discoverer and founder of Christian Science.

The longer I listened, the more entranced I became with the First Reader, a forty-year-old man with neatly combed blond hair, which, along with his white suit and black tie, accentuated a handsome, suntanned face. While he looked attractive, it was the vibrancy and conviction with which he read the passages from *Science and Health* that absorbed my attention.

I made up my mind to meet him. I practiced the theory that I could judge beliefs more comprehensively by talking to the men and women behind their convictions.

Two days later I walked into the First Reader's office and introduced myself.

''Doug, I was tremendously impressed by your service last Sunday. I was down that morning, and you lifted my spirits. I want to know more about Christian Science and, if you don't mind, more about you.''

He smiled, and with a mischievous twinkle in his eye said, ''To know more about me, you'll have to know more about Christian Science. But tell me first, how did Sunday's service lift you? I know you're a big real estate tycoon, and tycoons don't lift easily.''

I could see that Douglas was not the ultra-serious person I had pictured him to be. His sense of humor was dancing in his eyes, looking for an opportunity to perform.

''There's usually a good reason why tycoons don't lift easily,'' I said; ''you know why?''

''Sure. They're weighted down by mortal mind. But let's not get too serious. You were lifted. How?''

''By your joyous vibrancy. You read with tremendous conviction. What's the source of your fervor and, I might add, your sense of humor?"

"Divine Mind!"

I had heard those words many times, but not with the penetration and power with which he uttered them. I felt a strange force. He was reading my thoughts when he continued.

"*Divine Mind* are two innocuous words to those who are too busy to explore and experience their transforming power, but when one absorbs their grandeur as described in Mary Baker Eddy's *Science and Health*, a new vista of joy opens up. It sweeps away mortal mind's frustrations and anxieties. Confusion gives way to clarity. And what's so practical about Divine Mind is that we can prove its existence, its reality, its wonder."

"How?" I asked, fascinated by his directness.

"By demonstration. What's more convincing than proof?"

"You strike me as a stable, sensible individual—yet I'm puzzled. I'm a realistic businessman. How are you going to prove the existence of ephemeral Divine Mind?"

"I'm going to keep you guessing until Wednesday night at church." His serious serenity gave way to one of his mischievous smiles. "Please come. You'll be convinced that the little-used Divine Mind is a grander reality than the overused mortal mind."

A quarter to eight on Wednesday night, I was at the church waiting for the fulfillment of Gordon's promise. There were about a hundred people in the congregation, more women than men.

This time Douglas alone read biblical quotations and commentarial passages from *Science and Health*. It was a short, formal reading, and when it ended, Douglas turned to the congregation and said, "I now invite you to share your testimonies and remarks on Christian Science."

After several people in the congregation got up and told how they were cured of arthritis, bladder inflammation, eczema, and ulcers, Douglas announced his desire to conclude the evening service with his own story.

"While I was a junior in college," he began, "I was afflicted with cancer of the esophagus. Doctors gave me little hope. I hit the bottom rung of despair. My family and my Episcopalian pastor looked on helplessly. I quit school.

"A classmate of mine suggested that I see a Christian Science practitioner. I was skeptical, but desperate. I went to see one. When I finished relating my problem, the practitioner looked at me serenely, and without a trace of alarm said, 'There's no disease Divine Mind can't heal.' Then he added, speaking with authority, 'Divine Mind is the most powerful, the most scientific healing agent known to man, provided it is not merely believed, but *understood*. Understanding is the key—and diligently studying *Science and Health* will give you that understanding.'

"I bought the book and immersed myself in its beautiful prose, hardheaded logic, and above all its convincing arguments how switching from mortal to Divine Mind creates a radical change in mind and body. I read and reread the chapter on 'Fruitage'—the dozens of concrete healing examples. They sounded miraculous at the time, but what sounds miraculous to mortal mind is natural to Divine Mind. After I finished reading the book and attending several months of Sunday and Wednesday services, fear and worry left me, and with it the symptoms of cancer. My health was completely restored. This happened twenty years ago, and I haven't stopped expressing my gratitude to Christian Science ever since."

I now saw Douglas in a new light. Heretofore, I had been talking to people who were *explaining* religion.

He *lived* it, *demonstrated* it.

If he had been an emotional person who made implausible

claims, I would have dismissed him as an exaggerator; but Douglas was the epitome of stability, with the additional dimension of elegant dignity.

He intrigued me.

A week later I was in his office once more.

"Doug, I was bewildered by last week's healing testimonials, especially yours."

He smiled.

I continued.

"Was it the healing that caused you to change from an Episcopalian to a Christian Scientist?"

"That, and much more. Episcopalians are decent, respectable people. It's a fashionable religion, but too bland, too pat. Its pious platitudes never stirred me the way the difference between mortal and Divine Mind did."

"Tell me specifically how you changed from mortal to Divine Mind. It seems to be the centerpiece of your new religion."

"It is. Let me dramatize it. I stand guard at the gate of mind —turning back the so-called pleasures of smoking and drinking, the illusory satisfaction of revenge and snide remarks, and especially the fears and worries that used to churn my insides, which eventually exploded into cancer."

"Am I to conclude that by guarding against all negative thoughts, pristine Divine Mind takes over, and you become a radically different person?"

"You've got it. It's an exciting daily challenge, an unritualized religion that propels you faster toward God's ways because you don't have the rite and rote to slow you down."

"But isn't the church service a rite? And don't you work with the Christian Science textbook more or less by rote?"

"There is no ritual to the service. The readings are basically all that we do on the platform, and they take the form of lessons. The Sunday readings are, in fact, the same that Christian Scientists have been reading daily the previous six days.''

My friendship with Douglas resulted in my reading Mary Baker Eddy's *Science and Health*, attending several dozen Sunday and Wednesday evening services, and joining a Friday noon luncheon group, where Christian Scientists from several churches in the city met at the Milwaukee Athletic Club.

Douglas, of course, was always among them, gracing the table with his joyous wit and pleasant effervescence. But others were equally attractive: an owner of an auto parts business, a manager of a typewriter sales agency, a superintendent of a national food store chain, and varied business types. While most of the other diners in the large room were smoking, drinking, and conversing loudly, the Scientists' quiet joy was a serene contrast to the raucousness of their neighbors.

I was impressed by the difference and, of course, knew the reason for it. In one case, typical mortal mind was at work, while in the other, men were trying to express Divine Mind in action.

''There's no question,'' Douglas said at one of the luncheon meetings, ''that commercial remedies flashed on television, which claim to cure colds, actually induce more colds. Attractive people smoking and drinking in movies increase such desires in others. In fact, I know that manufacturers of cigarettes and alcohol pay movie makers to include drinking and smoking scenes for their subliminal imitative values. Violence, sickness, pornography shown on screens infect the minds of parents and their children. These suggestive influences are mortal mind at its roaring worst.''

''What's the answer?'' I asked. ''Most people would agree with you.''

''Would they? Some pillars of our community get more kicks out of discussing X-rated movies than discouraging them. The purveyors of alcohol, tobacco, and smut know it's bad—the evidence is overwhelming—but mortal mind keeps on driving them to do it. And mark my word, the next scourge that's about to engulf us is drugs."

"You still haven't answered my question," I pursued: "What's the answer?"

"You know what I'm going to say," he smiled. "Until people become aware that what they consider normal is actually abnormal, they'll continue to wallow in mortal mind's low-grade enjoyments."

"You sound just like Mary Baker Eddy," I said.

"I do? What a coincidence." His boyishness was cropping up again.

I didn't join their church. Becoming a Christian Scientist would have halted my search for a universal spirituality.

True, I've had a kind of spiritual love affair with Christian Science these last 30 years. But I've fallen in love with other views that have me equally impressed.

CHAPTER 7

Son of a Lutheran Minister Explores His Way to Unitarianism

Martin is a judge now, one of the finest in our city. When I met him 25 years ago at a Sunday morning Unitarian service, he was a young practicing attorney. His father was a no-nonsense Lutheran minister.

Durig the half-year that I attended Unitarian services, I got to know Martin, and I'm paraphrasing his story.

"Father," Martin began cautiously one evening, "I've become somewhat interested in Unitarianism and am thinking of attending a Unitarian service. How do you feel about it?"

"Not very good. I don't like to see you muddy your mind. You have a faith—a wonderful faith. Don't dilute it with theology."

"Isn't that strange coming from a minister—theology diluting faith?"

"Then let me be more specific. Your Lutheran faith isn't strong enough to withstand other ideas. *I* could go to a Unitarian service and not be affected, but you would be."

"What you're saying, father, is that your faith is closed, while mine is open?"

The minister's face reddened.

"That's a sharp-tongued remark, Martin, and I don't like it.

42

My answer is the same: I think you're making a mistake.''

"Well, father, I wanted to be completely candid about it; but I still intend to go.''

"I can't stop you physically,'' the minister said, raising his voice, "but you'll offend me. What will my parishioners think when they see that I can't keep my own son in the fold? They'll lose faith in me, as I fear you'll lose faith in your own religion when you begin dabbling in others.''

"I understand your feelings, but please try to understand mine.''

Accompanied by Jack, a Unitarian friend, Martin walked into what looked more like a lecture hall than a chapel. There was no religious art, not even a cross. The people in the audience were well dressed, and as Martin scrutinized several faces, he had the feeling that they were also well educated. After the congregation sang several hymns, an impeccably dressed gray-haired man walked up to the pulpit.

"He's one of the most successful industrialists in the city,'' Jack whispered.

"I'm a practical businessman,'' the speaker began. "I seek a rational rather than an emotional approach to God. I'm here because my common sense tells me that all religions are essentially the same. They stress the same virtues, and fall prey to the same vices. They stress love but divide themselves with hate. Unitarianism is an attempt to loosen dogmatic thinking, to cross religious boundaries, to seek parallel wisdoms, and not to be trapped into divisiveness. I use insights from many sources to improve my business. Why not seek God in the same way?''

This was a different view of religion from what Martin had been used to. Lutheranism had appealed to his emotions; Unitarianism was now playing on his intellect. This difference was given an additional boost when the minister, not much older than Martin, ended the service, not with a sermon, but with a talk on the need for United World Federalism. As a lawyer, Martin was impressed with the Minister's opening statement.

"The universe operates with precision based on laws laid down by a Universal Intelligence. Our efforts to live by law is reflective of that Universal Law. After centuries of struggle, we've reached a point in evolution where a person cannot impose his will upon another without being confronted by law. Yet, a nation, if it's strong enough, can impose its will on another with impunity. Why? Because nations are still living in a legal jungle, threatening and bullying each other as did primitive man."

Martin was puzzled by the secular content of the sermon.

"In the absence of international laws," the minister continued, "countries solve their differences by war. They've tried treaties and power politics, but these have only delayed the organized violence. Without enforceable law, personal relationships between people would be in shambles. As long as there's no enforceable world law, relationships between nations will remain as they are today—primitive. Our chance for greatness does not lie in exploring the moon. America's greatness lies in developing a United World Federation backed by world law and a world army, so that countries can be civilized the way individuals are civilized—by law. The world can no longer afford the luxury of an American dream, or a Russian dream—it must be a world dream."

Martin began to wonder what all this had to do with religion. His answer came when the minister concluded.

"Religion should have a double approach—individual growth and societal welfare. I would give priority to the first, only if it accelerates the good works of the second. They are mutually reciprocal."

"Jack," Martin said afterwards, "I've mixed emotions. The service lacked Lutheran warmth, but I must admit the businessman and the minister made a lot of sense, especially the minister's closing remark."

"I've been a Lutheran myself, so I know you must be full of questions," Jack said.

"My first reaction is that Unitarianism is too intellectual."

"True," Jack admitted, "but what's to prevent you from combining the intellectual with the spiritual?"

Martin attended many Unitarian services during the next several months, and he did a lot of thinking. He had one foot planted in Unitarian logic, and only his father's influence prevented him from putting the other foot there also. In fact, his father addressed the matter again not long afterward.

"This Unitarian nonsense has got to stop. It's gone far enough!" he exploded.

"Take it easy, Dad. Let's talk it over calmly."

"I've been calm long enough. You've become an embarrassment to me, and juicy gossip for my parishioners. You've had your intellectual exercise; now it's time you returned to your faith and stayed there."

"Can't we discuss this? Is your mind as closed as your religion?"

Martin was sorry the moment he said it.

"I can see how your new religion has infected you. You never spoke to me like that."

"I'm sorry, Dad. I shouldn't have been rude. But try to be fair. I fully understand why you want to hold on to Lutheranism. It's your life. But is it unreasonable to ask that you try to understand me? Why I want to reach beyond my religion?"

"You mean *away* from your religion," his father said icily.

"No, I mean *beyond*. What's so heretical about questioning? Didn't Jesus question, and Luther?"

"Don't put yourself in their places."

"Why not? Everyone has a right to question. I admit my questioning is not as profound, but within my limitations, I want to explore, too. I've found something that's changing my thinking about religion. Care to hear it? Not to change your mind but tell you why it's changing mine?"

"All right; what's so attractive about Unitarianism?"

"It combines faith with action. For instance, getting involved in creating a United World Federation, in defusing nuclear warheads, in promoting civil rights—this is spirituality at its finest."

"That's enough. It's social activism. It has its place—but it's not religion."

"Unitarianism balances other-worldliness with this-worldliness. Each reinforces the other."

"When you scramble them, faith suffers. Unitarianism will dilute your unique Lutheran faith in God, son. Let me tell you why." He was changing from firmness to conciliation.

"Just as individuals are unique, so different religions are unique. Nature is full of diversity; why not religion? Having one bland, united religion would miss the unique richness that each now contributes to our God yearnings. Don't dilute your heritage; add to its richness."

Martin felt the weight of his father's argument, and his thoughts sagged for a few moments. But not for long.

"The Lutheran uniqueness will remain with me. Unitarianism has merely exposed me to new thinking. Certainly one should have a choice to limit himself to one unique religion, but he should also have a choice to explore others. There's a new spiritual wind blowing across our land. It's realigning old groupings into new ones. Don't be surprised if one day it may even blow me beyond Unitarianism!"

I wasn't as impressed with Martin's Unitarianism as I was with Douglas's Christian Science or Matt's Religious Science. There was as much difference between the two as between the logic of ethics and the warmth of spirituality.

Social activism has its place, but it doesn't get down to the essence of being, the still center where God resides.

Martin was interesting. Douglas and Matt were spiritual.

PART III

Quantum Leaps from Atheism to Revolutionary Spirituality

Leaving institutionalized religion for a less structured faith is a forward step, but changing from atheism to spirituality is a quantum leap. The chasm is so wide that few cross it, and those who do become spiritual revolutionaries.

There are few uneducated atheists. The uneducated are more apt to fear God and not likely to reason themselves into denying Him.

The atheists are a motley lot who use all kinds of intellectualizations to deny God. There's the joy-ride type who is driven by hedonistic pleasure, with little concern for anyone but himself.

The epicurean atheist lives a genteel and agreeable life, seeking the best foods and wine he can find. He's affable, he bothers no one, and he is in total agreement with Epicurus' dictum: "The pleasure of eating is the alpha and omega of life." When asked to make a contribution to society, he's apt to quip, "That's not for me. I can't eat or drink it."

There's the intellectual monster who wears his atheism with proud arrogance. I met one of them at a Humanistic Studies Seminar in Aspen, Colorado. He was a professor who rudely cut off anyone who couldn't engage him knowledgeably on his level. He added a lot of cold knowledge to our discussions, but he lacked the warm camaraderie the rest of us enjoyed.

The ethical atheist, with a great deal of bravado, champions reason without faith, over faith without reason.

The most dangerous atheist is the zealous Communist. Oblivion-prone, he falls prey to the most inhuman expediencies. Stalin and his hordes were prime examples.

It takes a powerful idea to uproot an atheist.

But I've seen it happen.

It's a moving experience, as dramatic as a Hebrew Saul changing to a Christian Paul.

Chapter 8 shows how a small, unheralded group of men and women, under the aegis of Moral Re-Armament, are recycling barren atheists into spiritual revolutionaries.

And Chapter 9 examines the revolutionary transformation of a hard-hitting businessman who yielded, after a struggle, to the hard-hitting logic of J. Krishnamurti, an unusual, world-renowned spiritual thinker.

CHAPTER 8

Changing Human Nature
Is the Final Revolution

A WRITER'S MINDSCAPE IS CHANGED
FROM WEEDS TO ROSES

While on a family vacation trip to Mackinac Island, Michigan, I saw from a horse-drawn surrey a big sign reading MORAL RE-ARMAMENT. After my wife and three children were settled in their rooms at the Grand Hotel, I took a walk to investigate what was behind the sign.

When I knocked on the door of a large old rambling house, I was ushered into a spacious living room overlooking Lake Michigan, where a dozen men and women were engaged in leisurely conversation. Friendly black, brown, and white faces turned to acknowledge me. A few of them were in native costumes of foreign countries. I was politely introduced by a gentleman with an English accent to people from Japan, France, Germany, Burma, and Kenya. After we talked and I told them a little about myself, the Englishman invited me to have breakfast with him the next morning.

"I want you to meet Dick, a former feature writer of a slick New York magazine. You'll not only find him interesting, you'll grasp through him what we're trying to do here!"

49

After the three of us sat down for breakfast the next morning, Dick told the following story.

"My editor wanted a slick piece to show that Moral Re-Armament was a throwback to the Victorian Age. I holed up at the Grand Hotel with a couple of bottles of Scotch and began my interviews while an international MRA conference was in progress. For several days, the MRA people kept answering my cynical probes with a dignity that somehow began to blunt my cutting cleverness."

"What particularly impressed you?" I asked, my interest rising.

"They didn't quote the Bible. That attracted me."

"Why?"

"Because the Bible had little meaning for me. My parents attended church only because it was the respectable thing to do, and their apathy spilled over on me. I was clever with words, so after I graduated from college, I got a job with a magazine. I got pretty good at it, and better still at profligacy, with booze leading the way. What else was there? I was accepted by my peers because they found me interesting. We were sophisticatedly nice to each other when it served our purposes, ruthless as hell when it didn't. When I came here to write the story about MRA, I found an environment so different from my own that I began to probe beyond my assignment."

"What did you find?"

"I found God. It still sounds strange to say it, but it's the most direct way I can answer your question."

"What did the MRA people say that your minister hadn't?"

"Something altogether different. They asked me to try an experiment."

"What experiment?"

"They suggested that I remain quiet for an hour and listen to God before writing the article. It was an odd request, and for kicks, I thought I'd try it."

"What happened?"

"For about twenty minutes my mind kept churning my usual manipulative thoughts. Then a brand new one began to crowd in. I began thinking about how genuine the MRA people were, and how phony I and my friends were. I compared the quiet elegance of the women I met at the MRA conference and the women I knew in New York—the clever ones with their mask of flashy fashion. It dawned on me that these people wanted nothing except to change me into a better person, while I was maneuvering them to please my editor. I compared my selfish motives with theirs, my restlessness with their serenity, my drinking with their clear-eyed freedom, my drift from pleasure to pleasure to their joy of raising the quality of their lives and helping others do the same. As these thoughts crossed and recrossed my mind, I began to wonder that perhaps this is the way God talks to us—when we listen quietly."

"What happened next?" I asked, with increased interest.

"When I told a few of the MRA people what went through my mind during my quiet time, a banker who was among them said, 'Now that you listened and God has spoken, the only logical thing for you to do is obey.' "

"You're here," I said. "You must have obeyed."

"Yes, after several sessions of quiet times," he continued, "I began to obey and change—slowly at first, faster as the enormity of my change began to fill my consciousness. I came to stay a few days. I stayed six weeks. I went back to New York without the story, but a changed man."

"I've so many questions," I said, "that I don't know where to begin. Let me start with this one: Have you dropped out of your church?"

"No, but I don't find it as relevant as my new church."

"What new church?"

"The uncodified one I find in the privacy of my quiet time."

"How's it different from the church you reluctantly attended before you met MRA?"

"In many ways. I'm not distracted by people, I don't have

my communion with God prescribed by others. I listen to Him instead of reciting prayers and singing hymns. When I'm alone and listen quietly, God speaks to me personally in the form of thoughts. When they're lofty and unselfish, I know they're His; when they're shoddy and selfish, I know they're mine. During these daily quiet times, God has urged me to become honest with myself, to see the dirt in my life, and encouraged me to clean it up.''

''You must've done it. I see proof—the change from where you were to where you are. But have you personally been instrumental in changing anyone?''

''A few, but I'm still working on changing myself. We have a saying here: *The most effective way to change people is to start with yourself.* A changed person is a powerful catalyst to change others. That's why we have these conferences—bringing together people who changed, and those who need changing.''

MRA is not a religion. It's an international bonding of people who are looking for a common-denominator spirituality to raise the quality of their lives.

What they're doing is being done on a small scale against a big need, and they're proving what cynics don't believe—that human nature can change.

A HARD-CORE COMMUNIST DISCOVERS
THAT GOD IS THE FINAL REVOLUTION

Angelo was a hard-core Communist, writing marching songs for Palmiro Togliatti, Italy's number-one Communist during the 1950s and early 60s. I arranged a luncheon with him, his wife and daughter, and an interpreter during a Moral Re-Armament conference in the summer of 1955 on Mackinac Island, Michigan. Angelo was a thin, ascetic-looking man with dark piercing eyes—a revolutionary prototype. His wife was dark, short, and plump. His daughter, about twenty, studied me with calm, olive eyes. Victor, the interpreter, was an Italian American, fluent in both languages. From our outdoor restaurant table, we could see the peaceful panorama of the bright blue Lake Michigan waters meeting a pale blue sky far off on the horizon.

After we were seated, I asked Angelo, "What made you suddenly turn to God after years of ridiculing Him as the opiate of the people?"

Victor interpreted my question slowly, and as he did, I saw Angelo's darting eyes turn thoughtful.

"I was fighting Fascism all my life," Victor interpreted Angelo's answer; "yet all the while, I was a dictator at home. I never allowed my wife to question any of my decisions. My daughter feared me. I was fighting for the masses somewhere out there without relating the cause to my own family. I was tied to an ideological projectile. Then something wonderful happened. It opened my eyes."

"What was it?" I asked.

"What opened my eyes was something I never dreamed possible," Angelo continued. "A Christian Social Democrat named Primo, a rival of mine with whom I had had many heated political arguments, asked me to go to Caux, Switzerland. 'I want to prove to you,' he told me, 'that Communism is not the final revolution. There is something else.' I asked him what could be more final than Communism. 'Come with me and find out. The people there will change your mind,' he said. 'You mean I'll change their minds,' I laughed, 'before they'll change mine.' 'Why don't you come with me and find out?' he challenged. 'No one can change a Communist,' I said; 'you know that. You've tried for a long time.' 'I'm trying once more,' my rival said. 'Will you come?' 'All right, Primo,' I said; 'I'll go only for the satisfaction of proving you wrong.' "

Angelo stopped for Victor's interpretation before he continued.

"Smug and with a cynical chip on my shoulder, I walked into Mountain House Hotel at Caux with Primo, where to my surprise I saw people of many colors—black, white, yellow, brown—and in all kinds of colorful ethnic dress. Primo had kept much of what I was to see a secret from me—which is why I was surprised. That evening we had dinner with a banker from Britain, a dock worker from Brazil, a black politician from Kenya, a union leader from America, a French airline executive, and a German miner from the Ruhr. Primo introduced me as a Communist from Italy who wrote marching songs for Togliatti. I was ready for any adverse remark. None came. In fact, the English banker thought it was interesting to have someone who wrote marching songs for Communism, someone with a different slant on world problems. That surprised me, coming from a banker. The dock worker from Brazil added that he had been about to become a Communist himself, but had changed his mind when he came to Caux."

After another break, Angelo continued.

" 'What changed your mind?' I asked the dock worker. He replied that he had found a bigger revolution than Communism. 'What's more revolutionary than Communism?' I asked. 'Changing one's human nature, that's the final revolution,' he replied. 'What has changing human nature got to do with a political system that's superior to Capitalism?' I asked the dock worker. I was itching for a dialectical fight.

"The dock worker let the banker answer it. 'Changing human nature is more revolutionary than Communism. What good is any system if it puts ideology ahead of freedom?' I got the dig about freedom. 'Sometimes,' I said, 'it's necessary to curtail freedom when the people aren't ready for it.' 'Who'll decide when they're ready?' the banker pursued. 'Those who know,' I replied.

''The miner from the German Ruhr quickly reacted to my answer. 'To have to depend on those who know when to give people freedom is despotism. It's not reliable. There's a far more reliable guide.' I looked at the Ruhr miner with new interest. 'What's more reliable?' I asked. 'God's guidance,' he replied. I perked up, surprised. 'What's God's guidance got to do with meeting the needs of the masses? Have they brainwashed you here?' I asked sharply. I was up on my dialectical legs, ready for battle.''

Another pause, and Angelo continued.

'' 'No, they haven't brainwashed me,' the German miner replied. *'I was brainwashed before I came here!* You see, Angelo, I too thought Communism was at long last the final revolution. But I was wrong. Communism is new only in the way goods are produced and distributed. The difference between Capitalism and Communism is that in Capitalism, the people drive themselves and become greedy, while in Communism people are driven and become indifferent. That's why Capitalism outproduces Communism. But neither is the answer, unless we revive the forgotten factor that changes people and nations.' 'And what's that?' I asked, realizing that I was up against someone who not only knew what I knew, but knew something more.

'' 'The forgotten factor is God!' the German miner replied. 'We need a standard against which to measure the quality of our lives, and the most dependable and absolute standard is God. Now don't pooh-pooh it, Angelo, the way I did at first. It may sound trite and bourgeois, but it's still the most reliable standard we have to stabilize our lives. Sounds odd coming from a Communist, doesn't it? But Communism couldn't set me free—nor could any known form of government, unless I guide myself daily by listening to God. Try it yourself tomorrow morning. Listen. Ask God how you can become a better man, a better family man, a better *world* man!' "

After another interruption:

"All eyes turned on me. I looked around the group and didn't say anything for a long time. 'Don't try to draw any conclusions just now,' the banker finally suggested. 'Think about what has been said. Keep an open mind, and let's all meet for lunch again tomorrow.' "

Angelo's face was now flushed with excitement as he continued.

"I went to my room to wrestle with what had been said. Was this the beginning of a true classless society? Why did people of all races, religions, and nations gather here? I lit a cigarette and then realized that none of them had smoked during lunch. And none had drunk liquor. Then I remembered how often I had gotten drunk and had beaten my wife and thought nothing of it. I had excused myself because wasn't I fighting for a wonderful cause? What did a few personal missteps matter? I felt a slight pang of guilt. Could I have been wrong?

"These were intelligent men who couldn't have been easily hoodwinked into something that didn't make sense. I grappled with such thoughts most of the night, and in the morning I sat on my bed and tried to follow the miner's suggestion. I said to myself, all right, I'll listen, just to see what happens. My wife and daughter came to mind. I was a good Communist. But was I a good husband and father? Which was more important? If I didn't care for those close to me, how could I truly care for others away from me?

"For the first time, I became honest with myself. Was God talking to me, making me honest? Was He prodding my conscience? Is that what God's guidance is—waking up our higher

nature? Then I began comparing the men at the table with my
Communist comrades and with myself. They were relaxed,
we were intense. They valued honesty and unselfishness; my
comrades would think such thoughts naive and bourgeois.
They believed in polite persuasion, we in harsh discipline.
Which was the better way?''

Angelo now spoke slowly, more thoughtfully.

''I met them at lunch the next day, a bit shaken. Do I admit
to my wavering or hold on with pride to my ideology? Do I
forgo the praise for my marching songs, the friendships I had
built during twenty years of dedicated work for the Party?

''The Ruhr miner punctured my thoughts. 'You know what
came to me this morning?' 'What?' I asked. 'That you could
put your musical talent to writing inspirational songs for *us*—
songs about yearnings that transcend ideology.'

''Because I love music, he struck a response. 'Something
did happen during my morning quiet time,' I told them. They
listened attentively, thoughtfully, smilingly.

''Well, to shorten the story: I had planned to stay a day; instead I stayed two weeks. I met new people every day, and
each produced some change in me. I was becoming different.
I had found the Final Revolution.''

After lunch I took a long walk around the island to absorb
the thrust of Angelo's story. How was he different from those
who changed one religion for another? Or from men and
women I met at seminars on religion and international affairs, at United World Federation meetings, or at the Aspen
Institute for Humanistic Studies? They were learned men and
women who knew how to refine knowledge, but none had
Angelo's commitment to change. Most were spirituality som-
nolent. They were informed, but not inspired. They changed
opinions, but not hearts.

MRA sharpened my insight on the difference between those

who analyzed spiritual matters and those who actively did something about them.

It was an important spiritual lesson.

A MAU MAU TERRORIST HEALS
THE WOUNDS OF A NATION

Komo, an educated black of the Zulu tribe in Kenya, worked as a teller in a British bank during the day and terrorized English settlers at night. He was captured by British soldiers in a bloody raid and put into a prison compound with several hundred other terrorists.

A British officer who had been changed by Moral Re-Armament had requested permission of his superior to talk to the prisoners. After several denials, he was finally allowed to visit the prison with this warning: "Be careful. Don't get too close, or they'll maul you before you sound off your impractical dream."

When the officer walked into the stockade, the terrorists eyed him first with surprise, then with bewilderment, and finally with an intense curiosity for his next move. He raised his hand and introduced himself.

"My name is Norman Webb. I came here to apologize for my British arrogance—an arrogance that caused you to hate us. I'm sorry my government didn't pay more attention to your grievances."

It was a startling beginning—a Britisher apologizing to black terrorists! It gripped the prisoners' attention. He continued.

"Because we didn't listen, people were killed on both sides. But now that you're going to get your independence, let's stop hating, and help each other make a bloodless transition from our colonialism to your self-government. Let's build a peaceful Kenya."

"It's a trick!" one of the prisoners shouted.

"It's not. I'm asking you to rise above hatred. Blacks and whites can now join hands and reconcile differences."

Komo, who had been in captivity for several months, elbowed his way through the prisoners and stood in front of Norman. With the bearing of a self-assured, educated man, Komo asked:

"If this isn't a trick, what exactly do you want us to do?"

"I want some of you to join me in speaking before white and black groups, telling them that we need to forgive each other and together build a stable Kenya."

"We don't need the whites. We can build a strong Kenya ourselves!" a prisoner shouted. A mumble of approval rose from the rest.

"Hold on!" Komo shouted as he turned away from Norman to face his fellow inmates. "We have the numbers. The whites will be in a minority. We'll rule *them*, not they *us*. If they change, as this officer seems to have changed, why not use them to help us build our country?"

"I wouldn't trust him," another prisoner jeered.

Norman waited to see if others would come forward. None did.

"Let me explain an idea big enough to appeal to blacks and whites, an idea that empties hate-filled hearts."

Komo was still the only one ready to listen.

"What is this idea?" Komo asked, knowing he risked his comrades' anger. But he had taken greater risks, and he was ready to take this one.

"Come with me," Norman said, "and we'll talk about it."

A babble of disapproval followed them as they walked out of the compound.

"Traitor!" one of the terrorists screamed as the gate closed on the prisoners.

Norman's apology extinguished some of Komo's revolutionary fire. By admitting that the British might have wronged the

Kenyan people, Norman tapped the stable part of Komo that enabled him to hold down a responsible bank position. Komo was on guard waiting to see whether Norman's offer was genuine or deceptive.

After Norman explained how Moral Re-Armament had changed him, he persuaded Komo to accompany him to Caux.

Komo's heart beat with excitement as he and Norman collected their bags at Geneva and drove to Lausanne, twenty miles away, and then five more miles up the winding mountain road to the 800-room Mountain House Hotel, perched 5000 feet up on a cliff with vast sky above and luxuriant forest below.

During the month at Caux, Komo changed from a terrorist to a man of vision. He met former terrorists like himself who had become missionaries for change, former union leaders who put the power of God ahead of the power of labor, politicians with puny aims who changed to statesmen, corporation presidents who became as interested in people as in profit. And what gripped Komo's heart, mind, and spirit was that despite the great variety of cultures, races, and religions, all the men and women he met had a common aim—to live with a changed human nature under the guidance of God.

After Komo's exposure to a new kind of revolution, Norman and he were ready to take on Kenya as a proving ground for the practical implementation of Moral Re-Armament's vision.

They traveled up and down the countryside, appealing to blacks and whites to change from hate to conciliation. They spoke to unfriendly blacks and to equally unfriendly whites, and occasionally to mixed audiences. Their message was always the same—you cannot negotiate differences with past hatreds.

They would point to themselves, two former bitter enemies who had now become fast friends because they had discovered the healing power of forgiveness. Komo and Norman kept stressing that what they'd done, others could do, and then buttressed their appeal with the practical argument that the blacks needed the whites, and the whites needed the blacks, to build an independent Kenya, with equal rights for both.

Alone, Norman would not have been effective, nor would Komo, but together they became a convincing team. However, many of the hardened remained hard, a few of the stubborn became skeptical, and some of the skeptical began to change. Gradually, a mood of conciliation swept the country, and it reached Jomo Kenyatta, the number-one Mau Mau terrorist who later became president of Kenya. He issued several statements in praise of MRA, how it was moving his country toward a working relationship between white settlers and former black militants. As a result, other black-and-white teams were formed. Plays and movie documentaries attracted large mixed audiences. The theme was always the same—a changed human nature can change hatred to conciliation.

How Norman and Komo created the spiritual environment for the bloodless transition was related to me by a few of my MRA friends before the two were to appear on Mackinac Island in an MRA conference featuring the theme "How One Ordinary Man Can Make an Extraordinary Difference." About 500 people in the audience were eagerly waiting to hear their stories.

Komo spoke first. He was in his middle twenties, medium-sized, lithe, with intense eyes set in a blue-black face. Norman, standing alongside him, was a few years older, not much taller, a little heavier, blond, and serenely relaxed.

"I have a militant heart," Komo began, "and a militant heart needs an injustice to engage its passion. I found the injustice in the way Britain treated us. I became a terrorist. Revolutionary hearts are drawn to violence when there's no way to vent their outrage. I speak from experience. I had no higher aim than violence. Men like me have bloodied history.

"Tonight I want to talk about a new militancy, a new passion for justice that's more revolutionary and more effective than violence—a passion that lifts people to superior living. My friend here introduced me to it. After hours of discussion and many quiet times, I discovered that there are two kinds of passions: one drives to violence, the other leads to forgiveness. I've used both, and I know the difference. What a profound difference!" He stopped to take a few sips of water.

"We all know there are injustices in the world," he continued. "The crucial question is how to eliminate them. Unfortunately, too many choose the wrong way. In Kenya, I chose terrorism; I was driven by revenge. But I found there's a more revolutionary way to seek justice. It's not easy. It asks you to do what at first seems impossible—forgive those who wronged you. It takes a radical change of human nature to do this, and it's especially difficult when *you* have to be the first to change. At first, I was suspicious; but when I was convinced that Norman was sincere, genuinely interested in conciliation as equals, I agreed to listen to what he had to say, and eventually, I listened to what God had to say.

"I've talked long enough. There's no one who can explain the meaning of change better than the man who changed me, my friend to whom my country and I owe so much."

"I agree with Komo that it's easier to change when your enemy changes first," Norman began. "I was changed by someone I didn't like who apologized to me—and he had changed the same way. This chain reaction of change began all the way back with a man named Frank Buchman. He apologized to several people he vehemently disliked. They became his friends. He followed up this miracle of mutual change by launching, first the Oxford Group in the early 1920s, and then the worldwide MRA revolution in 1938. Thousands of people on five continents have radically changed their lives as a result of one man—Frank Buchman.

"In the years that followed, MRA men and women helped solve difficult personal, national, and international problems in labor, business, and politics. What Komo and I did was part of that MRA revolution, but it's minuscule compared to what needs to be done. The world's welfare will not be advanced with more knowledge, but with changed men and women who strive to rise above selfish human motives and eventually find their answers in God. Komo and I were atheists before we met MRA, and now it would be unthinkable for us to live without God's guidance. It was God's guidance during our quiet times that gave us the plan, the words, and the inspiration as we traveled up and down Kenya, to show by our example how hate between races can be changed to mutual help."

The audience applauded with a fervor that matched the zeal of the two young MRA revolutionaries.

A SWEDISH PROSTITUTE
TURNS INTO A MODERN MARY MAGDALENE

Ingrid was a go-go dancer from Sweden who left her country to carry on her stripping career in America. With no help or guidance from her divorced parents, twenty-year-old Ingrid relied on her curvaceous body to make her way in the new land. With no other skills than nude dancing, she was go-going in Los Angeles saloons with no other goal than using men for money and pleasure.

One day, Ingrid was introduced to Joan at the International House, a social agency where people from different countries met to discuss their common problems, living in a foreign land. Joan took a liking to Ingrid and invited her to lunch at 833 South Flower Street, where Moral Re-Armament had its West Coast headquarters.

Ingrid found herself in a strange new setting. Several dozen men and women were talking quietly at their tables. She noticed that none was drinking or smoking, and what puzzled her was that none of the women wore makeup. Her friend introduced her to several diners, but Ingrid's roving eyes were more interested in an attractive young man, and she made a few subtle feminine moves to gain his attention. He responded politely with a nod, but not in the manner of the young men she knew.

"Why do people meet here?" Ingrid asked.

"To help each other find God."

"Find God? That's for church, isn't it?"

"Some who don't go to church find Him here."

"Like me? I don't go to church."

"Yes, perhaps you."

Ingrid was losing interest in her friend's conversation and cast coquettish glances toward the young man who had caught her attention.

"Would you like a new plan for your life so you know where you're going, like the people in this room?" her friend asked.

"Where're they going?" This time Ingrid looked curiously at her friend.

"Let's talk about it during lunch with a few of my friends, including Don." She glanced at the young man who had attracted Ingrid's attention.

After lunch, in the discussion that followed, Ingrid was told that God has a plan for every individual, and that this plan becomes known if he or she listens to Him an hour a day and obeys the thoughts that come to mind.

"But how will I know if God has a plan for me?"

"When you're quiet and listen, God will tell you. The thoughts that come to your mind are God's way of talking to you," Don said.

Ingrid had never heard young men talk that way. Her interest grew.

"You mean if I listen, God will tell me what to do that's different from what I do now?" she asked, singling out Don's eyes.

"Exactly," her friend interjected. "Why don't you try listening to God tomorrow morning and see what happens?"

They talked for an hour.

Ingrid was as much interested in the sincerity of the people as in what they were saying. She compared them with the people she had known. There were no snide remarks, no lewd glances, no clever talk. Yet they were not boring. They were even humorous at times, and when she volunteered to talk about her entertainment world, there wasn't the slightest condescension or condemnation. She was impressed by their honesty, and gradually by what they had to say about God, about listening, and about how new ideas would come to her if she tried the quiet-time experiment.

The next day Joan, Ingrid, and two others were lunching at the same table.

"Well, what did you think about our discussion yesterday?" Joan asked, without pressing Ingrid whether she had tried quiet time.

But Ingrid volunteered, "I tried quiet time like you told me. I'm not sure if God talked to me, but I got an idea."

"What was it?" Don asked.

"That maybe I could find a better life if I gave up dancing in saloons. People there are not as friendly as here."

"Any other thoughts?" Joan asked.

"Maybe if I listen more, God will tell me what to do."

After several weeks of luncheon conversations, Ingrid said one noon:

"God told me to ask for a job here. I could wash dishes, clean, cook—I like the people here."

"But we can't pay a salary—only your room and board," Joan said.

"I'll work for nothing if you'll have me."

Ingrid moved into a small room on one of the upper floors of the center, and without being asked, gave up smoking, drinking, and makeup. After a year of diligent work, she told her friends that her quiet time "listening" was directing her to go to Mackinac Island, where she might be needed more than at the Los Angeles center. She compared her guidance with others, and they agreed.

Comparing guidance was a common practice among MRA people. When one had an important decision to make, it helped reduce human will, focusing more on God's will.

I met Ingrid on Mackinac Island at one of MRA's world conferences, where as part of the program, certain individuals were picked to tell their stories.

Ingrid appeared on stage in an authentic Swedish folk dress that accented her youthful, statuesque beauty. But as she began to speak, people became more engrossed in what she was saying than in how she looked.

"I come from a country of liberal ideas and liberal sex. My mother and father are divorced. I never went to church . . . I had no guidance from family or God. When I came to America three years ago, I brought the free sex idea with me. It only led to empty pleasure and deep sadness—until I met a friend who introduced me to MRA. Then something wonderful happened! I learned about the power of quiet time, and in reading the Bible, I found myself there as Mary Magdalene. She was saved by Jesus . . . I by MRA.

"I see a new kind of people in MRA—honest, happy people who listen to God. God talks to me too, when I listen. He tells me that sex is a gift for true love with one person, not a plaything with many.

"Now I have a plan for my life . . . and I can tell all unhappy young people that there is a way to be happy. I have found it . . . and so can anybody if one listens to God in quiet time. Thank you."

Several hundred men and women arose and applauded. As I looked around at the white, yellow, brown, and black faces, I could see expressions of wonder and approval.

I was moved too, as I was by Dick, Angelo, Komo, and others. Plunging into MRA work was an alluring temptation. But I held back. I gave them money, but not my time to the exclusion of all else.

I didn't want my spiritual evolution to end there.

CHAPTER 9

Nate Makes a Quantum Jump
to Krishnamurti

J. Krishnamurti, a world-renowned spiritual revolutionary, was giving one of his rare lectures at Ojai, California, a village nestled in one of the mountain ranges 80 miles southeast of Santa Barbara.

About a thousand people had gathered on a grassy clearing surrounded by a grove of oak trees to hear the eighty-year-old's radical views on how to transform today's society. He sat on a chair behind a bare table on a slightly raised wooden platform. Some in the audience were standing, others reclined on blankets they had brought along. It was early April 1976. A warm mountain breeze added a fragrant freshness to the scene. Except for a few curious newcomers, most were familiar with Krishnamurti's provocative views.

I had read some of his books, but Nate, my companion, had been a serious student of his for twenty years. When we sat down to lunch after the lecture, I was treated to an incisive explanation of Krishnamurti's wisdom by a man who had left his structured Catholicism for what seemed to me the ultimate in unstructured spirituality.

The marks of a hard-hitting, successful businessman were still visible in Nate's face and speech. Now and then a ner-

vous twitch of a hand or shoulder would slip into his otherwise serene manner.

"You're one of the few who really understand Krishnamurti," I began. "To me, he's still like quicksilver—now I
understand him, now I don't."

Nate gave me a knowing smile.

"When I first met his ideas, I too was puzzled. His thinking
was totally different from anything I had heard or read. But
when I penetrated his profound wisdom—and it took several
years—his shimmering views settled down into a rare order of
universal truth."

To get at the core of my puzzle, I zeroed in on what made
Krishnamurti most controversial—his total departure from
the world's Holy Scriptures.

"He talks and writes like an atheist," I said, to draw Nate
into controversy. "He thinks all religions are absurd, yet I
have a feeling he's reaching for a sacredness that's above
what's sacred in all religions. That's what puzzles me."

"Let's see if the sacred religious 'truths' which Krishnamurti uproots are really truths, or unquestioned fossilized beliefs which have caused so much havoc in the world. Shall we
talk about them?"

"Yes, go on."

"Devotion!" Nate stopped to emphasize the single word
before continuing. "The sages of the ages apotheosized it; the
world's Holy Scriptures glorified it. Yet, devotion followed to
its logical conclusion is not a virtue at all, but a vice. Why?
Because intense dedication to a religion leads to prejudice,
proselytizing, and violence. The religious devotion to holy
wars and today's fanatic fundamentalism prove it."

"I agree, but. . . ."

"Let me clarify the *but*. Holiness! A virtue? Not at all! Look
at all the havoc it's caused as the holiness of one religion
clashes with the sacredness of another. While religious leaders

dogmatize at the top, their different versions of holiness divide mankind at the bottom. Examples: the Middle East, Northern Ireland; I could go on.''

''Go on.''

''Tradition! A great virtue? No! A dangerous vice! The Wailing Wall in Jerusalem and Mecca in Saudi Arabia are hallowed symbols of tradition which have led to religions' divisions and violence. Tradition dulls, narrows, and clamps minds into straightjackets.''

''So far, you've downgraded the holy virtues. What about the secular ones? Are they vices too?''

Nate quickly changed gears.

''Ambition! It's warped decent men into egotism and insensitivity. How well I know! I've been there . . . felt its obsession. Ambition has been overmerchandized to the detriment of its worshippers and to the sorrow of its victims. At the end of unbridled ambition is a hollow abyss. Krishnamurti led me to it. I saw it, and turned away.''

I remained quiet—intrigued. He was interpreting Krishnamurti with a clarity beyond my own.

''Loyalty! A Virtue? No!'' he raced on. ''Intense loyalty to one idea screens out what's good in other ideas. Martyrdom is loyalty gone amuck. Remember, there are martyrs on both sides of confrontation. Loyalty is a vice.''

I now led Nate to what was uppermost in my mind. How would he interpret Krishnamurti's concept of God?

He again reverted to his habit of reciting a word, or phrase, and then explaining it.

''Seeking God! The greatest of all virtues? Not at all! When we pursue God with devotional petitioning, we distort Him. When we snare Him into an ism, we isolate ourselves from others.''

''Do you and Krishnamurti believe in God?''

''Not the way religionists believe. Only when we remove

the debris of ceremonials and dogma do we make room for God's Wisdom to enter our consciousness."

"What about seeking God's guidance? Would you call such meditation pursuing God?"

"Only when you wait for God with passive alertness does He come to you—quietly, silently."

"Aren't you playing with words? That's what I mean when I say that sometimes I understand Krishnamurti, and sometimes I don't. I have the same problem with you!"

"I'll admit that waiting for God after centuries of pursuing Him is not an easy concept to grasp. But when you do, a churning, divisive mind changes to a peaceful one."

"Let's put that aside for awhile," I suggested, "and get your thoughts on what Krishnamurti stressed this morning— the crucial difference between *functional* and *psychological* memory."

Nate stirred in his chair. I perceived it as a signal that he was about to make an important point.

"You're now getting to the very core of Krishnamurti's provocative ideas. Understanding the difference transforms violence to peace. Grasping the difference between functional and psychological memory has transformed me from an ambition-driven rogue to what you see—a peaceful man."

"All right; in a few sentences, what *is* the difference?"

"Psychological memory involves comparing, judging, condemning. These psychological seeds grow into needs for power, acquisitiveness, aggrandizement, hallowed tradition, and remembering to settle scores for past injustices."

"Be more specific."

"For instance: I'd never forget an insult or a curve someone threw at me. I'd slip it into my psychological memory. When the time was right, I paid it back in spades. Nations have psychological memories too. Israel remembers Jerusalem and the Wailing Wall. West Germany will remember East Germany.

The scattered Armenians and Kurds are still remembering the land that was theirs. All these psychological memories spawn hostility and violence. What used to drive *my* psychological memory was wanting more, striving for recognition, and getting ahead of my competitors. With nations, it's patriotism, honor, aggrandizement. With religion, it's tradition, holiness, dogma. In individuals and in nations, these memories become psychological boils that grow, spread, and rupture into violence.''

"Before you explain what Krishnamurti means by functional memory, how does he suggest we get rid of psychological memory?''

"We block out our psychological memories when we begin observing instead of opinionating, comparing, and condemning. Easy to say, difficult to practice. But it can be done. When we stuff our minds with strong opinions, we close them to new ideas. When we compare, someone is hurt. When we condemn, someone's going to get even. When the same kind of psychological maneuvering spreads in a nation, it leads to sloganizing, propagandizing, arming, and violence. Unless the psychological genie is put back into the bottle, psychological memories will run, and eventually ruin, our civilization.''

"How's Krishnamurti's revolutionary wisdom going to put the psychological genie back into the bottle, when the Sermon on the Mount hasn't done it?''

"Just as a garden has to be hoed, so spiritual wisdom has to be restated. Jesus did it for his time; Krishnamurti is doing it for our time.''

"Are people listening, changing?''

"Very few. His thinking is too advanced, too subtle for people who've been psychologized by religion, sterilized by reason, intellectualized by Freud, and hedonized by ambition.''

"All right, that's enough for psychological memory! What about functional memory? Anything wrong with that?''

"Nothing! Functional memory creates order, promotes progress. Remembering mathematics, how to drive a car, bake a cake, or meetng a train on time doesn't get us into trouble. Functional thinking is an orderly process, just as the laws of nature are an orderly process. Krishnamurti has made us aware of the profound difference between psychological and functional memories—a mighty spiritual contribution! Philosophers and religious thinkers have yet to come to grips with it. I could talk about it for hours, but I think we've talked long enough."

I tried to fit Krishnamurti into my master plan of spiritual development.

He didn't fit, and it disturbed me.

After months of quiet-time wrestling, I resolved my problem with the answer that just as there's an essential unity in diverse religions, so there's an essential unity in varied sources of spirituality.

Fitting the pieces together into a spiritual, cohesive whole became a purposeful, ever-changing challenge.

PART IV

The Good and the Bad
of
Religious Fundamentalism

Dare we gamble with ridding ourselves of doctrinaire religion when hundreds of millions depend upon it for their religious sustenance?

But shall we remain stuck in straight-jacketed orthodoxy, when the bias of the pious eventually leads to violence?

It's a dilemma. The pluses and minuses of institutionalized versus uninstitutionalized religion pose a disturbing conflict. We can reason ourselves in or out of either proposition, with equally convincing arguments.

Reaching for God is a primal yearning, and to organize this yearning is as primal as the yearning itself.

But arrayed against organizationally fixed primal yearnings is a more basic law—the law of spiritual evolution. It culls, it sifts, it disturbs; and always, because of its great wisdom, only the more suitable forms prevail. When a minority vision becomes more suitable for the advancement of evolution, it becomes the majority.

The majorities and minorities will always be with us, as they keep succeeding each other.

Our problem today is whether to yearn with the religious majority or the spiritual minority. Both reach out for the same God.

That's the uniting factor.

Their differences are the dividing factor.

The challenge to both is to live in mutual tolerance, relying on the law of patient evolution to work its way without resorting to recrimination and violence.

CHAPTER 10

The Mindscape of a Fundamentalist

Al had one foot on earth and the other in heaven. One was in a bank, the other in his church.

I was one of his mortgage customers. In our dealings I had found him fair, firm, and honorable. His mind was like a steel trap, opening and closing on financial matters with springlike speed.

Before I met him, I dealt with Al on the phone several times a month when unusual problems arose. We developed a warm telephone friendship. I was at the peak of my busy career, and I tried to solve as many problems over the phone as was practically possible. I suppose he was in the same position.

One day a burly, jovial man walked into my office and asked for a real estate salesman's job.

"Have you had any experience?" I asked.

"Some. You've got a busy office here, and I learn fast. I'm sure I could do a good job for you."

The more I questioned him, the more interested I became. He was genial, handsome, confident. Just as I was beginning to raise my hopes about hiring a great find, my visitor burst out laughing.

"George!" he boomed. "This is your phone buddy—Al! I thought it was time we met. Now, I know, should I ever lose my job, I can always work for you," he quipped.

I had talked to that voice dozens of times, and now that it had materialized, I was startled. When I recovered from my surprise, I said, "Al, you son-of-a-gun, you fooled me completely!" I got off my chair to shake hands. "I had no idea you were so big!"

"Six-feet-four."

"That's a lot more than my five-feet-six!"

"More important, George, is the bigness of the inner man. I've heard you're searching for some new kind of religion."

"And I've heard you're a deeply religious man."

"My religion is more important to me than my business. It's no accident that my three daughters are nuns."

This drew us quickly into a discussion. I told my secretary to hold my calls.

"You know, Al," I began, "I think we're seeing the twilight of old religions. They've served their purposes. We're entering an era of unifying spirituality, a toning down of divisive religiosity."

"George, you may be a practical real estate man, but you're an impractical dreamer if you believe what you've just said. Unless, of course, all religions will be universalized into Catholicism. But I'm realistic enough to know it won't happen. As of now, we need the old religions more than ever, to keep our civilization on track. To stop the erosion of character."

"*You're* the impractical dreamer, Al. Do you think the religious leaders of Islam who are preaching a Holy War against Israel, and the religious leaders of Judaism who want Jerusalem to become their eternal city, are ever going to transcend their dogmatisms and advance civilization beyond their own beliefs? No, Al. It will come from people who will conceptualize God in a more vital and believable way. Their universalist gospel will usher in a new spiritual age. It won't come from the vague conjecturings of old religions."

He listened quietly, but then almost in anger came back at me.

"I want to correct your misconception about what you describe as the vague conjecturings of old religions. I'm a Catholic. I don't conjecture about God. I know! What I believe couldn't be more definite and positive."

"All right, Al, what is your future role with God, after death?"

"I'm going to be resurrected with the second coming of Christ and live in bliss forever," he said without a moment's hesitation.

"In the flesh?"

"Yes, in the flesh—and forever," he emphasized.

"In what kind of body?"

"In my present body."

"That's definite, all right, but not very scientific. Let me ask another question. Are you one of those fundamentalists who believe that the world is 6000 years old? In the parting of the Red Sea? In the Immaculate Conception? In other words, in the literal interpretation of the Bible?"

"Yes, with all my heart—something you can't do with all your vague universalism. Let me tell you something, George. If you don't stand for something, you stand for nothing! You're all over the lot. Too many options are a curse, not a blessing."

"I'm amazed that you can be so logical in business and so illogical in religion. How can you stick to your fundamentalism in the face of modern scientific findings? Carbon measurements show that the earth is billions of years old, and skeletal evidence shows that man has been on it for millions of years. Do you still believe that Eve came out of Adam's rib?"

"I'm more interested in what *I* believe than in what *scientists* believe. I know that what I believe fills me with love for God and love for man. As on earth, so in heaven; there's always a reckoning. And I want to be ready. Now how about *your* rationale for leading an exemplary life? What are *your* ideas about life hereafter?"

"I part with you when you stop at a permanent heaven to stay there forever. For me, life is a constant becoming, not one resurrection like yours, but endless resurrections in the form of endless reincarnations. We're both after the same thing but conjecturing differently."

"But your conjecturing is a fantasy, it's not in the Bible. Anyway, go ahead . . . you might as well finish your fiction."

"Brace yourself for something you've probably never heard before. Man dies three times before he is reincarnated into another life. First he dies physically and enters what is known as the astral plane. This can best be described as an emotional level of existence where finer energy atoms than our gross physical atoms become the body of our consciousness.

"After a life span of less or more than a hundred years, depending on many variables, we die on the astral plane and enter the mental plane, a body of still finer atoms where our consciousness is immersed in mental energy. After another hundred or so years, depending upon the lessons learned from previous incarnations, the monad or permanent atom, which gathers and individualizes the wisdom of all the previous planes of existence, develops an urge for more experience in another physical incarnation. It then enters another human body, never in a lower life form, and usually in one whose vibrations are similar to the one seeking another incarnation.

"The monad or Soul which enters the new body comes with all its previous propensities—good and bad. That's why we have child prodigies and people with little talent, people who are foolish and people who are wise, each Soul pulsating with the urge for more spiritual experiences. Those who are aware of this reincarnational sequentiality—always keeping in mind that this process is a perpetual movement Godward—have a more plausible concept of God than those who believe in stopping at some ephemeral heaven, taking all the ignorance with them that still needs many incarnations to process into spiritual wisdom. For me, all this is more plausible than the vague speculations of priests and rabbis.'' I stopped and looked at my visitor.

"Well, Al, does all this give you something to think about?"

He looked at me for several seconds.

I could see that he was against everything I said.

"I hope I won't hurt your feelings—you've worked so hard to explain yourself—but I think it's all a lot of rubbish, George. Do you think people will buy your bizarre concoction against 2000 years of organized Christianity put together by some of the greatest minds of all time? Or against the Hebrew religion of 5000 years, or the Muslim religion of 1300 years? You're a gnat against an elephant!"

"Or a David against a Goliath?"

"Except in this case, David will lose!"

"Al," I said, striking a conciliatory note, "obviously we're not going to convince each other. While we don't burn heretics at the stake any more, you'll have to admit that the old religions are still clinging to differences, causing dangerous and unbridgeable divisions."

"Not divisions, just differences. It's natural that people should disagree on the most important concern of their lives. Why are you so concerned about differences?"

"They're not just differences, Al; they're fierce divisions that kill people. I'd trust men like you as heads of religious orders—but, unfortunately, too often charismatic leaders rise to the top and whip unthinking followers into frenzies that defy reason. They warp spirituality into cruel, grotesque religiosity. It happened before. It's happening now."

"George, let me end this conversation on a personal note. You're restless. If you had my belief, your restlessness would end. You'd be a happier man—like me. You may judge me as a man of blind faith, but I judge myself differently—a man committed to God, without any of your restless searchings. I believe in the old and enduring. You're fiddling with the temporal and unreliable."

"Al, despite our differences, I admire you. I admit your religion has molded you into an honorable and good man. We come from different directions, but we meet on a plane of reasonableness. Yet one-on-one reasonableness is blown to the winds when haloed leaders get in the act and blow up religious divisions into violence. That's what disturbs me. That's what happened in the past and is happening now."

"You're disturbed because you're mixed up with the new. I'm at peace because I rely on the old."

We shook hands and he left.

Al posed a disturbing obstacle to my unfolding spiritual evolution. If an intelligent, worldly man like Al could not erase his religious conditioning, what hope was there for the less intelligent? If Catholicism were threatened, wouldn't Al be swept up with the ruling hierarchy and do its bidding?

I wondered.

CHAPTER 11

How a Rabbi's Orthodoxy Limited His Spiritual Vision

It was not a particularly busy afternoon. When my secretary buzzed to announce that a rabbi wanted to see me, I said, "Send him in." I didn't know who he was or why he was calling, but an encounter with a wise rabbi, I thought, might enliven an otherwise dull day.

He looked like a Jewish Rasputin in his black gabardine coat and long, luxuriant black beard. His eyes were dark, deep set, but friendly, unlike the Russian's fierce mien. He kept his wide-brimmed black round hat on when he sat down to face me.

"I've come to see you because I understand you're Jewish."

"I'm Jewish, but in a way you may not approve. How can I help you?"

"To be brief, I'd like a big donation to buy a house in your city. We need a place to spread information about the Lubavitcher Jews."

"Who are the Lubavitcher Jews?"

"You're a Jew, and you don't know?"

"No, I don't."

"We're an orthodox group who are trying to bring back to the fold those who have strayed from the original biblical Jewishness."

83

"Why should I give a big donation to something I don't know? Besides, I have some ideas about orthodoxy I'm sure you won't like."

"Like what?"

"I think narrow orthodoxy, in whatever religion, keeps people divided. For instance, orthodox Jews have little to do with people of other religions, or even with Reform Jews."

"Don't talk to me about Reform Jews! They're a bunch of *goyim*. They've watered down biblical Judaism to where it's meaningless. That's why Rabbi Schneerson in New York wants every city in America to have a nucleus of Lubavitcher Jews to attract others to the way God meant us to live."

"Let me ask you, rabbi: as wonderful as the original concept was, don't you think we can improve on it after so many years?"

"Can you improve on God?"

"That's too simple an answer. Jewishness is not God. I'm suggesting that perhaps we can improve on ways to commune with God. How do the Lubavitchers know that what's written in the Bible is the only way, the only truth?"

"Because it was written by men inspired by God."

"Wasn't the New Testament also written by men inspired by God? And isn't it possible that men today can also be inspired by God? Isn't it logical to assume that God hasn't stopped sending his inspirational impulses to help us understand Him?"

"There are no new ways to improve on our Bible."

"Not so. Many of the customs and rules that prevailed among the Jews centuries ago are irrelevant today. You still want women separated from men at synagogues, not to mix meat and dairy products, and a host of other antiquated religious rules that don't fit in the twentieth century. Please don't be offended, but your dress makes you look like you've come out of the past. To make religion work, we need to move forward, not backward."

"What's forward?" he asked challengingly.

"That spiritual wisdom is not limited to Judaism. Other insights, when blended with Judaism, form a more comprehensive view of God than when it's narrowed down to one dogma, whatever its name. Doesn't that make sense?"

"My dear man, you've bitten off too much—you'll get religious indigestion. I've got enough religious enlightenment in Lubavitch to keep me God-inspired for the rest of my life. I don't need another religion. You may be smart in business, Mr. Bockl, but not about your religion. You should know that one wise, authentic belief is better than many dubious ones, and Lubavitch has it."

He sounded like Al, the devout Catholic banker. Despite the similarity of their fundamentalist yearnings, their different beliefs, rules, and ceremonies keep them apart.

"You're a fine and honorable man, rabbi, but with a major defect. Your God's wisdom doesn't stretch enough to cover more of humanity. Your beliefs divide people—Lubavitcher from Reform Jews, Jews from Christians, Jews from Arabs, and so on. Wouldn't it be more spiritual in the eyes of God for Arabs and Jews to stop clinging tenaciously to Allah and Jehovah, and together worship the same God? Wouldn't such wisdom transcend the narrow beliefs which foolishly keep them apart? The more the Lubavitch orthodoxy and Islamic fundamentalism try to be different, the more they divide and kill. Wouldn't building bridges between them please God more? Save lives?"

"You're asking for the moon. You're too ambitious, not practical. You're trying to change the world. I'm less ambitious. All I want is to provide a Lubavitcher home for young Jewish boys and girls who've been on drugs, with gurus, Moonies, and so on. Also, we hope to bring back those who've fallen away from orthodoxy back into authentic Judaism. You're spraying your shots and likely to hit nothing, while we're on target reconstructing lives."

I was about to tell him what's being done on a world scale by Moral Re-Armament, Theosophy, Christian Science, Religious Science, and the like, but changed my mind. He was too steeped in Lubavitcher lore, and too engrossed with his house project, to have it make a dent in his convictions. Instead, I zeroed in on his remark about spraying my shots while he was reconstructing lives.

"I agree that we have a moral obligation to the immediate, and I commend you for it, but we can't stop there. We must also be concerned about posterity—to heal the festering religious wounds."

The rabbi looked at me with a puzzled expression.

"I don't know what to make of you. I can't say you've fallen away from God, but it does seem you've fallen away from Judaism. What are you?"

"I try to glean spiritual wisdom wherever I find it—from the Bible, Buddhism, any well-thought-out spiritual view. In a profound sense, they all merge into One. That One describes me best; the composite is where I find the most direct line to God—in the essential Oneness of spirituality."

"You'll lose yourself before you'll find yourself. You're on a dangerous quest."

"But this dangerous quest is the hope of the future. It's already begun, and its wisdom will eventually silence the discordances of today's Tower-of-Babel religions."

I stopped.

"May I digress a moment?" I resumed.

"Go ahead."

"Do you have a marriageable daughter?"

He answered a quizzical "Yes . . ."

"What would you do if she married out of your faith?"

"I'd disown her," came the swift reply.

"Even if a gentile would stack up better than a Jew?"

"I'd still disown her. But it could never happen. She's as much a Lubavitcher as I am."

"Isn't it because you drilled it into her?"

I mentally kicked myself for turning the discussion into a debate.

"You know what prompted my offensive remark?" I retreated. "It was my recent reading of *Brothers Ashkenazi*, where it describes how the Hassidic Jews of Poland used to drill their children in strict orthodoxy to keep them in the fold. I presume the Lubavitchers do the same."

"Since you still read Jewish literature, I'll not only forgive you, but admit that we have to instill Lubavitch wisdom into our children if they're not to stray the way you did, and get lost the way you did."

I let his conclusion pass without comment.

After we sorted out each other's thinking for another twenty minutes, the rabbi asked the practical question for which he had come to my office.

"Despite our differences," he said diplomatically, "can I depend on your generosity in proportion to your means and get a substantial donation for Lubavitcher House?"

"I hope I can phrase my refusal as graciously as you've made your request. I have donated hundreds of thousands of dollars during my lifetime to both Jewish and non-Jewish causes, much of it toward helping break down walls between religions. However, if you'll be satisfied with a donation of a few hundred dollars, I would be willing to partially honor your request."

"I want you to give with your heart. A token donation won't do. I'd rather take nothing than a token. Don't be offended. I understand your reasoning, and I hope you understand mine. Now, I'd like to leave with a story.

"A young man, whom I'm sure you know, used to date your daughter while they attended the same high school. When he graduated from college, he joined the hippie crowd because he found no heart-fulfilling answers from his Reform Jewish parents. While they gave lip service to their watered-down

Judaism, he became a despairing atheist. He bounced from commune to commune, went to India in search of a guru, and finally, between bouts with marijuana, became a devotee of Alan Ginsberg, whose poem 'Howl' became his pagan bible. He was a lost soul, searching for something to hold on to when someone suggested he see me.

''What followed was a miracle. As the young man put it, 'I've found my true home at last.' He returned from his wanderings to the authentic Judaism which has held us together for 3500 years. His despair dissipated. He became a vital, happy young man. He's married now to an equally happy young woman who, like her husband, had returned from her undisciplined wanderings to the inspired discipline of Lubavitch living. His name is Marvin Kane. I thought you'd be interested to know what happened to him.''

I thanked him for sharing his story, and he left.

Indeed I remembered Marvin Kane. His story and the Lubavitcher rabbi dredged up contradictory layers of thinking in me. Certainly the rabbi was doing meritorious work—rescuing young men and women from rudderless lives. He, like Al, and millions of other good and honorable men and women, were disciplined by their Holy Scriptures to lead commendable lives. But because these good people are dogmatized differently, they separate themselves from each other and create the conditions for future clashes.

It's not easy to give up a conditioned good for a potential abstraction. The immediate exerts a greater pull than the future. But we must steer a middle course—keep one foot in the present and the other in posterity. Otherwise we stunt spiritual evolution.

CHAPTER 12

How the Islamic Religion Cast a Cold Shadow on Warm-hearted Muslims

David was a wholesale grocer with an annual $10 million sales volume. He was known as a "good guy" in his industry because he helped many small struggling retail grocers get on a sound financial footing.

When Palestinian Arabs emigrated to his city and started small grocery stores, they flocked to David for guidance and financial help. He gave it to them with friendly abandon, and because they didn't know he was Jewish, they clung to him both in business and as their best friend in a foreign land.

Many invited him and his wife to dinner. They told him about their five prayers a day, their tithe, their strict fast, their pilgrimage, why Mecca and Jerusalem were holy to them, and how peaceful life was in America compared to the turmoil they left behind.

When the Palestinian grocers learned that David was having his seventieth birthday, they invited him and his wife to a celebration in one of their small social halls. About thirty families, dressed in their best flowing Arab robes, gathered to pay homage to their benefactor.

First one, then another got up, in their halting English praising David for what he'd done for them. When the last man had spoken, they waited for David to reply.

89

David was moved by their goodwill. He had rarely been appreciated in so warm a manner. His wife had tears in her eyes. A thought slipped into David's mind that now was the best time to reveal his Jewish identity. He got up and with some trepidation began to speak.

"My friends, you honor me with a warmth I have seldom experienced. What I've done for you, you've repaid tenfold with your friendship and, I might add, with your business. You are among my most loyal customers. I value your patronage, as you seem to value my service. It's a mutual partnership."

He stopped a moment for the punch conclusion.

"And now I have to tell you what's been on my heart and mind for a long time. I earnestly hope it's not going to disrupt our trusting relationship. I am Jewish."

A shock wave swept through the audience.

They gasped in disbelief.

After a stunned silence, there was a mumbling in Arabic among the men and women. One of the grocers got to his feet, and in a trembling, confused voice said, "I feel like rock hit me on head. Jews drive us out of our homes. Jews not good to us. Now you. . . ." and he sat down.

Another got up.

"I sorry. You good friend, but now. . . ." He raised his arms and shrugged his shoulders.

The women and children stared at David but said nothing. With a sigh, David once again addressed his friends.

"You and I are victims of religious hatreds. Ali . . . Ibn . . . Abdul . . . Ahmed—you are all my friends—it's sad that religion should come between us. I knew you were Palestinians when I dealt with you, but I didn't discriminate. I befriended you. I helped you. Why can't we remain friends?"

Abdul, who seemed to be their spokesman, rose to his feet and, nervously straightening his headgear, said:

"We talk about problem . . . let you know."

The brevity of Abdul's response struck a portentous note. Gone was his usual volubility. David's revelation had dredged up traditional divisiveness and cast a pall on the festivities.

After David related this story to me, I asked, "Then what happened?"

"First one, then another, then all quit dealing with me. We come from the same root race, but because something went cockeyed way back, we're killing each other in the Middle East and poisoning peaceful friendships here."

"Got an answer to this?" I asked.

"Intermarriage!"

"What? Are you serious?"

"Yes I'm serious! Treaties, Arab terrorism, and Israeli counter-strikes are as doomed as rearranging deck chairs on the *Titanic*."

"How would you feel if your son married an Arab?"

"I don't know about my son, but if I were twenty-five today, I wouldn't mind marrying some of the Palestinian women I've met. They're gorgeous! My religion wouldn't stop me."

Several months after David lost his Palestinian customers, he attended a recognition dinner honoring a woman for selling the most bonds for Israel.

"I attended that dinner," David told me after a golf game, "because I still consider myself a Jew—but a liberal, pluralistic Jew, one who draws no lines against any religion. After they finished praising Esther, the honoree, I called her aside.

" 'Esther, you're an intelligent woman. You've a good grasp of world affairs. The Jews are honoring you for helping the Israelis. But nobody is honoring anybody for helping the Jews and Arabs to live peacefully the way people of different religions live in America. How are we ever going to solve the Jewish-Arab problem?'

" 'Not by doing business with them, the way *you* do!' Esther shot back. 'Your business is more important to you than Judaism. My mother would call your kind of Jew an *apekarus*, and I'd agree with her.'

" 'And building walls of hate is a better way?'

" 'All I know is that they're our sworn enemies, and I hate enemies,' she charged. 'And by the way,' she asked, 'how would *you* solve the problem?' "

David turned to me with a grin as he continued the story.

"I shocked her when I said, 'Intermarriage.'

" 'Wash your mouth, you *apekarus*! Only an enemy of the Jews would talk like that!'

"I told her that half the Jewish marriages in this country are with gentiles, and not all Jews are wringing their hands about it. And these gentiles are more removed from the Jews race-wise than the Arabs.

" 'With Jews like you,' she flared, 'we'll never build a strong Israel. You are a traitor to your own religion!' She left in a huff."

"What's to be done," I asked David, "when good people like your Arab friends, and an intelligent woman like Esther, refuse to look wisely at their common problem? If *good* people won't bend, then what hope is there for *fanatics* on both sides?"

"Well, you're writing about these things, and I'm trying in my small way to put them into practice. It'll take a long time for even the good people to see the light, and perhaps centuries before the zealots come to their senses."

"Why are there so few like you, and so many of the others?"

"Because we're a stiff-necked people, and the Palestinians, who're related to us, have the same defect. Look at Switzerland. The French, Germans, and Italians shed their nationalities and became Swiss—and now live peacefully together. Wouldn't it be wonderful if the Jews, Palestinians, and Jordanians federated into a canton-type Greater Palestine? It would be risky for the Jews. They would become a minority canton, but it might be less risky than being surrounded by tens of billions of armaments and hundreds of millions of Arabs.''

"You had better not suggest your canton plan to the Jewish leaders, or you'll be excommunicated like Spinoza was centuries ago.''

"They're not going to excommunicate a mere grocer who's still giving to Jewish causes. You see, I still have one foot in Judaism—but the other is in the future, hoping for the time when we'll have some type of federated Palestine.''

"You're a new breed of man, David. There's hope when more like you will be as concerned for the future as they are for the past.''

CHAPTER 13

The Paradise Promise of Jehovah's Witnesses

When John got out of military service in the 1960s, he had neither a goal nor the ability with which to carve a niche in society. Without a job and with too many empty hours, he was frittering away his life.

One day, a young man and woman came to his door and handed him a small magazine with the title *Awake*.

"What's in it?" he asked in a surly manner.

"It's about how to lead a happy life on earth, and how to live forever after the resurrection," the young woman replied.

"Forget it! I'm not interested in either." John started closing the door.

"Mind telling me why?" the young man asked pleasantly, trying to keep the conversation going.

"Because there's nothing here to make me happy, and living forever is a pipe dream."

"But what if God guarantees it—wouldn't we be fools not to take advantage of it? I talked just like you until someone showed me how wrong I was. If you give us a few minutes, we'd like to tell you what we've learned and why we believe it's true," the young man pursued.

"If you want to waste your time, go ahead," John said, inviting them in.

They were trained Pioneers, volunteer workers for Jehovah's Witnesses who knew how to spot a lost soul and what to do about it.

With a persuasive sincerity that grew out of an unswerving conviction, first one, then the other, probed John with questions and then promised that living the life of a Jehovah's Witness would guarantee him a job. The job guarantee aroused his interest.

"What do you mean, I'd be guaranteed a job—?"

"This is what we mean," the woman Pioneer hurried on. "When you change into a Jehovah's Witness, you will become a different, more desirable person. Employers will recognize it. They're always looking for stable, dependable workers. There isn't a committed Jehovah's Witness who is out of work. Believe us, it would solve your job problem."

John's interest grew.

"What do I have to do to become a Jehovah's Witness and be guaranteed a job?"

"All you have to do is study the Bible with us for several months. From that study you'll get the inspiration to lead a good life."

"What do you mean—'a good life'? What do I have to do?"

"Very simple. Don't drink, smoke, use drugs, or carouse. Instead, make up your mind to help your brothers and sisters in any way you can."

"I don't have brothers or sisters."

"All people are your brothers and sisters. Show them care as we care for you. Turn your back on Satan, who urges you to be mean, which makes you unhappy. Employers don't like mean, unhappy people. That's why you're out of work. Please believe us, it's really that simple."

"You mean if I lead a good life, it will make me happy, and then I can get a job?"

"Yes, but to become happy and stay happy, you have to believe with all your heart that there's a big battle going on right now between good and evil, between God and Satan, and that those on the side of evil will be destroyed. You see, when you decide to fight alongside God—and we can teach you how—you'll lose all your meanness, all your unhappiness. You'll become a caring person, a Jehovah's Witness, and you'll have the best of two worlds: happiness right here and now, and the promise of everlasting life. Two huge rewards if you decide to battle Satan alongside God. And we can help you become that happy warrior!"

"Where do I learn more about this war you're talking about?"

"We'll come and study the Bible with you each week. It'll open your eyes to an earthly Paradise, a new way of life, a caring for people—and a job."

They stressed the job angle, because from practical experience they had learned that satisfying a pressing need accelerated the proselytizing process.

The Pioneers ignited a spark in John's heart, and the literature they left behind fanned it into a flame.

After several months of study with the woman Pioneer, John became a Jehovah's Witness, and a regular attendee of services at Kingdom Hall, the name designated for their churches all over the world.

By a juxtaposition of incidents, I hired for a secretarial job Marlene, the Pioneer who had trained John to become a Jehovah's Witness. Several months later, when there was a maintenance job opening in one of my buildings, she suggested I interview John. I did and I hired him, not because of his experience but because of his courteous manner.

I learned a great deal about Jehovah's Witnesses from Marlene and John. When John invited me to a Kingdom Hall lecture, I accepted. I wanted to see what made Marlene and John so content, so serenely peaceful.

The lecturer spoke for an hour, followed by questions and answers for another hour. I was impressed with the audience participation, but I felt uncomfortable with the endless quotations from the Book of Revelation about the last days on earth, about Armageddon just around the corner, and about Jesus' coming to rule the Earth for a thousand years.

The lecturer stressed that those who believed would enter Paradise, but those who didn't would be destroyed, without any chance of redemption, because it's either Paradise or oblivion. The lecturer cited the Bible as the scientific proof of the coming events. He who doubts the Bible, he ended, is lost forever.

I looked at the congregation. The majority were plainly dressed, and I surmised that most of them were below the economic middle class. I liked what I saw in their faces—friendliness, spontaneity, credulity. Blind belief gave them a glow of innocence.

But while Marlene received many compliments from my business visitors for greeting them with unusual geniality, and John was appreciated by my tenants for his genuine caring for their minutest needs, both had developed defects because of their total commitment to their religious views. Marlene bristled when she heard me discuss Theosophy with some of my visitors.

"It's none of my business," she blurted out one day, "but isn't Theosophy against all religions? You don't act like an atheist, but doesn't being against all religions make you an atheist? I'm confused."

"Let me unconfuse you," I said. "I'm not against all religions. I'm interested in *uniting* all religions."

"You know that can never happen."

"Why not?"

"Because we don't even agree with our first cousins, the Catholics and Protestants."

"What don't you agree on?"

"A lot of things. We think their pompous churches, graven images of Christ and Mary, and their elaborate ceremonies are all idolatrous. God will judge us only on our simple, lovable deeds, not on our show-off religious ceremonies.''

''Aren't you too hard on them?''

''Not when we disagree on fundamentals.''

I could see that I touched the deepest root of her belief, and I backed away from further discussion.

John's commitment to his job was exceeded only by his fanatic commitment to Jehovah's Witnesses. He became the best maintenance man in my organization.

That was the good part of John.

But there was a bad part developing alongside the good.

He had separated himself from his Baptist family. He shunned their birthday and Christmas ceremonies. Eventually, he became a stranger to family gatherings.

Underneath his courteous caring for people I detected a strain of intolerance. He gave the impression that he was dealing with sinners—the natural reaction of one emotionally sure of his strong beliefs.

But could Theosophy or Krishnamurti have done for John what Jehovah's Witnesses did?

Obviously not.

John was on an emotional plane, perhaps several incarnations away from the spiritual plane, at which point the never-ending Godward journey accelerates.

CHAPTER 14

A Physician Reconciles the Contradictions between Science and Religious Orthodoxy

Every Friday before sunset, Melvin drives his family from his palatial home in an exclusive suburb to a dinky flat in a shabby neighborhood one block from an ultra-orthodox synagogue. This enables his family to walk to Friday night and Saturday morning temple services. He doesn't drive during the twenty-four Sabbath hours, work, or use the phone. From Friday's sunset to Saturday's sundown, he does nothing but rest, meditate, and pray.

Melvin is chief of internal medicine, with a specialty in endocrinology, in a large hospital. He enjoys an outstanding reputation in medicine and in his community. He is a tenant in my medical office building, and I stop in occasionally for a friendly chat.

"You puzzle me, Melvin," I observed one day during a lull in his office. "I can't understand why you observe the Sabbath with all its meticulous biblical traditions."

"Because I think playing golf, listening to a football game, or carrying on business as usual, the way most Jews do, is a violation of God's law. Besides, from a medical standpoint, I can tell you that there's great therapeutic value in clearing the mind of mundane noise for one day, and letting your affairs rest on God."

"I go along with the therapy reasoning, but why would a modern scientist like you want to adhere to primitive religious rules? You don't rely on primitive medicine. Why primitive religion?"

"I have a simple answer. I want to renew Judaism in its pristine form, in its original one-God wisdom that has civilized the world. There's your answer, direct and to the point."

"It's neither direct nor to the point, Melvin. You haven't met me head on. Why use the latest in medicine and stick to the oldest in religion?"

"Because science is different from religion. Science deals with matter, religion deals with spirit. The yearning for God 3500 years ago was the same as it is today. Why sully it with modern garbage? Don't you think an original is better than a copy?"

"Were the original medicine men better than the modern doctors?" I persisted.

"You're not getting the point, George. The original medicine men dealt with matter. They were primitive scientists. We've improved on them. But have we improved on the wisdom of the prophets? on Moses? on the Psalms? I don't think so. I don't find any awe or mystery in the slick Reform sermon or in any of the new-fangled changes in modern Judaism. I love tradition . . . antiquity . . . the ancestral yearnings of years gone by. I get inspirational shivers running down my back when I hear bearded men chanting, or cantors singing. They awaken a genetic response in my Hebrew psyche. I get emotional. Divine Jewish spirit has not changed; it doesn't have an expiration date. I got goose pimples when I worshipped at the Wailing Wall several years ago. I could feel the ancient spirit murmuring in my blood. I was where it all began, and from where it spread to the world. I wanted to feel the way the ancient Jews felt, to experience God the way they did. Are you beginning to see the difference, George?"

I had a subsequent talk with Melvin's father, who was a successful lawyer and a good friend of mine.

"Tell me, Ray, why did your Melvin veer off into ultra-orthodoxy? I can understand why he might follow in the foot-steps of an orthodox father—but you're an atheist."

"From your point of view, I suppose, a *no-good* atheist!" he quipped. He was proud of his sharp-retort reputation.

"No, be serious. Why has Melvin turned his back on your atheism and embraced fundamentalism?"

"He hasn't turned his back on *me*. We get along fine. He's found something that neither you nor I have—religious secu-rity. I don't need it, and you don't have it. Otherwise you wouldn't be groping for your visionary universalism."

"I know you don't agree with my ideas, but do you agree with his?"

"I don't agree with either of you. I'm as much perplexed at his orthodox antics as I am with your cockeyed views. Both of you are reaching for skyhooks. I'm more practical, down-to-earth. I'm neither an angel nor a devil. But Melvin is differ-ent, very different. He's all angel—but a stubborn one. He won't deviate one jot from his orthodoxy. His way-out kosher rules, wearing a yarmulke in public places, and a host of other inane religious rules are driving me nuts. But he leads an ex-emplary life, far superior to mine. His marriage is built on a rock, his patients adore him; and without pushing the way I do, he makes more money than I. When I'm beset with doubt —not often—I sometimes get the uncomfortable feeling that perhaps Melvin's crazy orthodoxy is what made him the fine person he is. I tell you, George, he's a puzzle. I don't under-stand him."

I had another talk with Melvin after my discussion with his father.

"Your enviable character convinces me that the individual fruits of fundamentalism are good. What bothers me is that when fundamentalists like you stick to your orthodoxies, and fundamentalists of another ism put a halo on theirs, the stage is set for trouble. That's the dangerous dilemma that cries out for a practical solution."

"I'll help you resolve it."

"How?"

"Reconcile yourself to the fact that there'll always be religious differences. There're all kinds of differences in nature; why not in religion? I'm not bothered by Christian, Buddhist, Muslim, or any other faith so long as they'll let me have mine. Be honest, George: don't you agree that statistically speaking, you'll find finer character among fundamentalists than among watered-down religionists or atheists? Why? I'll tell you way. We're close to the Source—where the Original inspiration bubbles through our veins. Could you fire up a God-inspired storm among universalists? If your Emersonian ideal had any spiritual validity, don't you think it would have caught on by now?"

"If I read you right, you're primarily concerned with your own salvation. But what about the safety of the Jews in the future? By remaining zealously different, they become a target for tomorrow's frenzied fundamentalists of another religion."

"Are you suggesting assimilation—God forbid—?"

"I'm not suggesting assimilation into another religion, or giving up ethnic differences. We want diversity. But wouldn't the world be a more peaceful place if fundamentalist leaders of all religions assimilated their religious differences into a transcendent spirituality? Their separateness is irreligious, sinful. The evidence is so clear that clinging to each one's holiness leads to violence. Why not give up narrow religiosity for transcendent spirituality?"

"And forget our history, our covenant with God that made us special? That's what our Reform rabbis and people like you are doing who don't practice the wisdom of the Torah, who don't internalize the holy fact that we're the Chosen People. The nonorthodox are demeaning Jewry by giving lip service to being Jewish, but not practicing what makes them Jewish. You can see what's happening to our assimilated Jews. They're becoming carousers, drunks, Moonies. But not those who hew to the Hebrew scriptures. Can you compare Emerson's intellectualizing to Moses' Ten Commandments, or to the religious thunder of our biblical prophets? Universalism can only lead to bland uniformity. It wouldn't have a devotional grip. It's a pabulum religious feeling—no passion, no fervor, no sacred wisdom, no vision to pass on to our children. Your universalist God is an abstraction."

"Not an abstraction, but a vibrant Universal Intelligence that I've personalized into the same I-Thou God relationship that you're worshipping, but without the orthodoxy that would separate me from others."

"You're reaching for skyhooks, to use my father's expression."

"And you're cemented to hopelessness when you cling to the negative proposition that the melting down of fundamentalism is impossible. I view it as the next evolutionary step towards a spiritual renaissance. My vision is broader than yours. It embraces more of humanity. It has that extra dimension yours doesn't: no divisiveness."

"George, you're hooked on an impossible dream. My religious security is real, built on time-tested wisdom. Yours is ephemeral—built on sand."

"No, Melvin, yours is built on the past, mine on the future."

CHAPTER 15

Born-Again Christians
Are Good People—But . . .

Floyd is as suave and handsome as Jerry Falwell, who is his idol. But unlike Falwell, who speaks quietly, Floyd comes on like the black bull in one of the major liquor ads.

I was invited to dinner and an evening of discussion by a group of born-again Christians. There were eight people around the table, and Floyd was their spokesperson.

"We invited you to be our guest,"Floyd began after dinner, "because of your articles regarding some esoteric views about religion. While your strong stand against pornography, gambling, and general moral decay parallels ours, you seem to drift off in some sort of universalism, diluting your otherwise good arguments. Would you clarify yourself?"

"Sure. What do you want to know?"

"I'll get directly to the point," Floyd pursued. "It seems you're taking a fuzzy route to what we both want—a Christian America, free of the secular garbage that's rotting our country. Isn't that so?"

"I agree with what's rotting our country, but I don't want a Christian America. You do—I don't."

"Why not?" Floyd's face reddened.

"Because I'm for *spiritualizing* America, not Christianizing it."

"But it's the same thing: when you Christianize, you spiritualize!"

"But why *your* way? How would you like it if others tried to Judaize, Hinduize, or Muslimize America? Don't you see, when you Christianize, you're dividing; when you spiritualize, you're uniting."

"Look, you're a man of action. We're familiar with what you've done in real estate. You're practical. You know how to get results. If we're to get the dirt out of our country, we've got to be practical too—use what works. Christian evangelism *works*. We're changing millions into God-abiding citizens. Never mind the Bakker or Swaggart affairs. They're aberrations, the breakdown of two or three people, not of our gospel. We'll come out of these fiascoes stronger than ever. We'll continue to reach millions of hearts, while you'll be dawdling with a few minds. We're practical; you're dreaming.

"There's a real estate aphorism," I said, sparing them the Bakker and Swaggart embarrassments, "which goes something like this: Don't be in a hurry for the quick buck; instead plan prudently for long-range success. The Ayatollah Khomeini was against the moral decay of his country too, but instead of taking the slower and more enduring spiritual course, he went for the quick fix, and you know the rest. Your quick conversions could be edging toward his hurried approach."

"Don't compare us with the Iranians," one of the group spoke up heatedly.

"No, not you people; but what if one of the star televangelists became a Superstar? What if he played on the emotions and made putty of fifty million viewers who now pay two billion dollars a year to watch the electronic churches? What if using the Power and Glory of God with showbiz flair catapulted him into the presidency? What then? What if this religious fundamentalist hero, with the genial tube manners and granite resolve, thought that he was chosen as a messenger of God to turn America into a moral Christian nation? Or change

the world? I'm not suggesting that this superstar would perse-
cute minorities the way Khomeini does—but who knows?
Dare we take a chance?''

"Wait a minute," Floyd cut in, "you're getting carried
away. We're dealing here with decent preachers who only
want a clean, moral America. If you're for their values, as you
say you are, you should be grateful that they're doing your
job. The evangelists are merchandizing morality with imagination, and that's why it's selling.''

"That's the danger," I cautioned; "they're obsessed with
selling. Religion is too important in our lives to be sold like a
product. When faith is hammered into people, it changes into
fanaticism, loses reason. Charismatic television preachers
who offer books, prayers, calendars, lapel pins, and what-nots
are huckstering for the dollar with the same hard-hitting selling schemes that are used by the most hustling businessmen.
The evangelists preach morality, but what about the immorality of self-aggrandizement, the driving ambition to be Number One on television, the histrionic ploys to get more money,
to get more prime-time television—and, yes, build mansions
and drive expensive cars with the dollars out of the pockets of
poor people—?''

"But all this money is used to get more people into the
ways of Jesus Christ. What's wrong with that?'' Floyd asked
with a tinge of anger.

"The end doesn't justify the means. That's the Soviet way,
not ours. Selling religion on a hacienda set with orchestra,
singers, and live audience is a vulgar way of inspiring people.
That's not religion. That's entertainment.''

"You're exaggerating," Floyd said. "What counts is results.
Decent people are flocking to Jesus. The proof is right here in
this room. Each of us is a born-again Christian. We're free
from the rot that's blighting our land. What has universalism
done? How many people has it inspired? How many are living

better lives because of your esoteric stuff?'' Floyd's face flushed with triumphant excitement.

"You've got me on numbers,'' I admitted. "You're getting results—but I'm afraid, dangerous results. The good could turn ominous if the religious exhorters succeed in Christianizing the Supreme Court, convince Americans that liberals are Communists, religionize our schools—in other words, veer toward a theocratic society. That wouldn't bother you, but it would bother me.''

"How would *you* change America?''

"By sounding the alarm that unless we remove religious walls between fundamentalist religions, we'll continue to wallow in divisive human misery. You may not know it, but there's a network of people in some sixty countries using such diverse names as International New Thought Alliance, Theosophy, Unity, Religious Science, and many smaller groups without any recognizable names, who are aiming for the long pull of a global, nonexclusive, undogmatic spiritual family without distinction of race, creed, or color. They don't promise to turn "scars into stars,'' the way evangelists do. But they're trying with a passionate faith in God to lay a more durable foundation for people of all races to live in a less divisive world. They're not spectacular, but neither is spiritual evolution—it sweeps slowly and majestically.''

"Fancy words, George,'' one of the other participants joined in. "Your way would take a millennium to right what's wrong with society. We need change *now*.''

"Would Jesus anchor a religious variety show even if he knew that he could reach every household in America? I don't think so. St. Paul, maybe, but not Jesus.''

"I think he would,'' Floyd said, "if it was the most effective way to reach and preach the gospel to millions.''

"Friends,'' I said as we all stood up to leave, "obviously we're not going to agree or settle this momentous question.

However, I want to thank you for inviting me. All of us here believe in God—that's what unites us. How we do it—that's what divides us. Until our differences are resolved, let's remain tolerant of each other. I'm sure that would be God's way.''

There are many faces of fundamentalism. They vary with each religion. But fundamentalism has two constants: it's quiescent and pro-life on an individual basis, but often virulent and anti-life on a collective basis.

PART V

The Good and the Bad
of
Secular Humanism

Several decades after Ralph Waldo Emerson espoused his universalist spiritual manifesto, Robert G. Ingersoll formulated his credo about humanism. "Humanism," he said, "should be based on the bare bones of fact, not on the myth of supernatural authority."

It's true that secular humanists have used the bare bones of fact to fashion just, courageous, and generous lives. But it's also true that by limiting themselves to the *merely* human, they miss the spiritually fulfilling experience of knowing God.

CHAPTER 16

A Composite View of
Secular Humanism

THE TYPICAL* PROFESSIONAL MAN OR WOMAN

I was having lunch after a round of golf with three of my friends—a doctor, a lawyer, and a businessman.

"George," the lawyer said, "you're making too much fuss about religion. People are talking about you! They don't understand why you're writing books about some sort of universal spirituality instead of sticking to your own religion. Why don't you let the professional clergy do their thing, and you do yours? This is an age of specialization, George. You're trying to stick your nose in someone else's business!"

"Look, guys," I said, "we all know how to make a living— but shouldn't we also be interested in *how* to live, how to develop a master plan for our lives?"

"Sure," the businessman said, "but what's that got to do with what you're talking and writing about?"

"*Everything*! The old religions are becoming virulent

---

*It's always crude to generalize. What is "typical," after all? Still, there are *types*—we see and meet them every day. Generalizations have value, provided we don't use them as an undiscriminating dragnet. There are plenty of exceptions, and long may they live!

111

again. To protect our children's future, shouldn't we try to mute fundamentalism, to flush it out of the world's civilization?''

"You talk like the Communists," the doctor spoke up. "*They're* trying to do away with religion too."

"But I'm suggesting something different. The Communists are out to eradicate religion; I'm interested in *revitalizing* it. What I'm talking about is a worldwide spiritual renaissance that challenges the atheists and gung-ho religionists to replace their too-much religion or no religion at all with the revolutionary concept of *God without religiosity*. This new approach is more scientific than fanaticism and fills the vacuum of atheism. It's more important than adding another layer of success to our careers."

"I think learning how to get out of a sand trap is more important than all of this," the lawyer quipped. "Seriously, this esoteric stuff is not for us—at least not for me. We're decent humanists. What more do you want?"

"It's not enough, fellas. Humanism is too bland. I grant you it's easier to reason with humanists, especially nice guys like you, than with blind-faith fundamentalists. But a rational belief in God beyond today's vague abstractions can make your lives more fulfilling. I could go on, but I can see you guys aren't interested."

"To be honest, George, you've taken the correct temperature of our interest," the businessman chimed in. "We respect religion, but we don't fuss about it." He turned to the other two at the table. "Wouldn't you say that about sums it up?"

They agreed.

I was disappointed, but not surprised.

The change from the familiar to the new is a difficult one. It takes a major shift of attention before we recognize the reality and feel the pull of the Universal Intelligence. It's a subtle experience. It requires remaining linked to the mundane, yet being able to vault over it.

THE SOCIAL SCIENTISTS

Psychiatrists, psychologists, teachers, and social workers are generally secular humanists. A leading psychiatrist in our city was a tenant in my office building. We often brainstormed in my office, away from his desk and couch.

"I know you're getting some of your patients out of their abnormalities, and that's commendable," I said. "Dredging up the past and draining off poisoned memories are apparently helpful. But what about *spiritual* therapy—an inspirational healing that lifts us beyond the mind, beyond psychiatry—?"

"That's a fuzzy area. We know more about the psyche, how it works, than about spirituality or its inspirational value. If your mind got off the normal track, wouldn't you be grateful if I could put it back on?"

"Yes; but is adjusting to a particular cultural norm enough? Wouldn't relying on an Invisible Wisdom prove more dependable than psychiatry, make cures stick? Don't some of your patients fall in and out of cures?"

"I don't mix an Invisible Wisdom with psychiatry. Psychiatry is a science; God is an abstraction, an unprovable theory. Yes, some of our patients do fall in and out of cures, but you must remember: years of wrong thinking take a long time to heal. You can't do it with a hocus-pocus God procedure. That's not scientific. I deal with the mind, with what we know; not with what's beyond, what we don't know. That's for visionaries like you," he ended with a friendly smile.

"How about Jesus? Didn't he reach beyond the mind and cure physical and mental ailments? Isn't metaphysical God Wisdom more powerful than your laboring therapies that stick for a time, then get unstuck because they're limited to the mind?''

''Well, what about the Ayatollah Khomeini, who kills with the same God Wisdom?''

''Don't equate Khomeini with authentic pro-life prophets. He's off the wall. Prophets cleanse our minds with a more powerful solvent than the one you use to dissolve dirt in our subconscious.''

''It looks like we can't convince each other,'' the psychiatrist observed, ''so stick to your Invisible Wisdom, and I'll stick to my psychiatric science. Should you get lost in the wilderness beyond the mind, my couch and I will be waiting for you to find your way back.''

''And should your mind reach a dead-end, there's spirituality to get you beyond it. We both know that our psyche is like a fragile plant, easily starved of purposeful nourishment. And when that happens, it becomes a rootless tumbleweed, driven aimlessly by mental winds.''

He gave me a benign smile.

Reason is the rock upon which humanists build stable lives. They fall off now and then, but they usually climb back on.

I come from the world of reason. It's not bad, not good. Getting into spirituality is like moving from two- to three-dimensional living. You see more, feel more, enjoy more. It's no visionary fluff.

BLUE AND WHITE COLLAR WORKERS

Blue and white collar workers tend to focus their interests on their families, jobs, and recreation—in that order—with only a dutiful nod to their churches. Few are familiar with the difference between religiosity and spirituality. Perhaps more than half of our hundred million work force belong to the same elbow-bending fraternity—the blue collar wage-earners meeting regularly at their saloon haunts, the white collar employees at their cocktail lounges.

They drink the same stuff but vary the gossip. The blues discuss their athletic heroes; the whites, their favorite entertainers.

Having built hotels, office buildings, and apartment complexes, I got to know carpenters, electricians, plumbers, construction workers, as well as the white collar personnel that round out a building project. They're fine, decent men and women, but uninterested in—and therefore woefully uninformed on—the difference between petitioning prayer and spiritual prayer. The petitioning kind looks for Someone without—the spiritual, for God within.

The wage earners' absorption in their daily affairs blocks out serious interest in anything beyond.

This is not a criticism.

It's a fact.

No wonder that when I posed the question "What's your most important goal in life?" to several dozen blue and white collar workers, most of their answers were:

"Make a living for my family."

"Educate my children so they can make more than I do."

"Work at something that's a joy instead of drudgery."

"Get a kick out of life."

Meritorious goals, but they fall short of higher aims, such as:

"Change the world for the better."

"Uplift rather than diminish people."

"Seek ways to be an instrument for good."

Despite our prosaic aims, America has the most stable stock of people on earth. Our ethnic, racial, and religious diversity is our strength. One group does not have enough influence to dominate the others—in contrast to Germany, where its monolithic population launched its monstrous experiment to purify its race.

Our diverse religions, which have tamed themselves ecumenically not to snarl at each other, have played no small role in humanizing us into becoming the world's foremost democracy. We can preserve and enrich this democracy if our churches ecumenize their religiosity into spirituality and infuse into our growing number of aimless people values that transcend the pompous exclusivity of denominationalism.

ARTISTS

Artists, as a rule, have little interest in religion. Their work is their God. Nor do they have any interest in the skulduggery of business or in what interests the white and blue collar workers. Their art isolates them from mainstream activity and, as a result, they develop introverted, ivory-tower personalities—obsessed with their work and removed from what goes on ''below.''

Many of the artists who climbed to fame during the last fifty years slid off into amorality. Whether their lifestyles reflected their art or their art was influenced by their lifestyles, the bottom line was that much of their literature had veered off to pornography, music to raucous rock, and painting to riots of violent shapes and shouting color.

Instead of elevating culture, they have coarsened it.

Instead of stimulating our sense of beauty, they have stunted it.

Perhaps Nikos Kazantzakis, the world-famous Greek poet who lived through half of the turbulent twentieth century, had the answer for the artist's plight. Wallowing in the existential trough of Sartre and Camus, wavering between despair and detachment, Kazantzakis finally fulfilled his life when he accepted the reality of spirituality. There, he said, he found peace.

When I suggested Kazantzakis' discovery to a few of my artist friends, one of them said:

"I've heard of him. He was all over the lot—unconventional, despairing, rebellious, Communist—and then he fell into religion!"

"No, not into formal religion, but into universal spirituality. It was the final answer to his thrashings for meaning."

"All right, have it your way. You're not an artist, so you don't really know what goes on in our minds. We're intemperate humanists. Our unrestrained personalities are what differentiates us from the herd. We build our own world, and I assure you, it's more exciting than yours."

A not-so-gifted poet who supported himself peddling watermelons off a truck told me that fashioning ideas out of words to express his innermost feelings meant more to him than marriage or worldly goods.

Like the typical artist, he couldn't balance his obsessive interest with normal living.

Artists may argue that their function is merely to reflect their culture—what's good and bad. Unfortunately, the good is smothered under an avalanche of bad—violence in movies, vulgarity in literature, cacophony in music, disfigurement in painting. The primary interest seems to be in the sensational grab for attention.

Art should aim at elevating our human aspirations to lead sensitive lives. Artists shouldn't get away with the excuse that "what is" is more important than "what should be." That's not art; that's journalism.

Our minds are constantly taking pictures, and these impressions stick to our mindscape, condition our thinking, and eventually either disort or balance our mode of living.

Artistic humanists owe us more than riotous, sensational individualism.

SCIENTISTS

Few scientists are churchgoers. Their minds are honed on physical reality, not on biblical mythology. Scientists are usually more disciplined than artists, because they deal objectively with things, while artists involve themselves subjectively with ideas.

Scientists don't stray from normal cultural behavior. The main thrust of their lives is to advance knowledge. They're humanists to the core—with this defect: they're more interested in the physical than in the metaphysical, more interested in their specialized knowledge than in society. With objective indifference, they shower us with useful goods, and with the same unconcern they load us with world woes— nuclear Frankensteins, chemical poisons, and now genetic engineering.

I tracked the career of a typical scientist. At college, we studied physics together. He was brilliant. He became a college professor with a doctorate in physics.

When I saw him in the mid-1980s after many years, he was a picture of professional grace, a white goatee matching a full head of white hair. He was still as slim as I remembered him, with the same lively, intelligent eyes. After reminiscing for an hour, I asked, ''How do you feel about genetic engineering? Do we develop or scrap it? Even some scientists warn us that we're overreaching ourselves here.''

''Science must advance no matter where it takes us,'' he said evenly.

''Even if it threatens havoc to the race, with mere mortals playing God?''

''Science should pursue generic engineering, otherwise we'll never really know what it's all about, what it can and cannot achieve.''

"You sound like an Edward Teller, who pushed for the hydrogen bomb, not like Robert Oppenheimer, who opposed it. I had hoped you were an Oppenheimer."

"Oppenheimer ceased being a scientist when he became a visionary."

"Don't you think we need more visionary scientists for mankind's sake, rather than more insensitive scientists for science's sake?"

"George, I knew you weren't cut out to be a scientist when we studied together, and I'm afraid that's still true."

"And you, Oliver," I said with a smile, "are still as one-pointedly objective as you were—but more dangerous."

Scientists are speeding myopically ahead—and their secular humanism seems to be in too high gear to stop their dangerous race.

THE TYPICAL MEMBER OF MAINSTREAM RELIGION

The majority who attend church services do so more out of habit and respectability than out of any fervent conviction that they're linked to God. They're not really much different from humanists.

"If I were to be startled by a stranger in a dark alley," a church-attending friend of mine told me, "I'd feel safe if he were a humanist or the average churchgoer, and scared if he turned out to be an atheist."

I agreed with that observation. Religious values humanize.

However, it takes a heavenquake to spiritualize.

One of the signs that we're going through a heavenquake is when we change from loving only when we're loved to the spiritual way of loving even when our love is not returned.

"I'm fully aware of the weaknesses of church religion," the

same friend told me; "but in all honesty, I'm too comfortable to want to get out of it. I guess I'm genetically programmed to stay in. Years of Catholicism have dinned it into me. I'm intertwined with the rhythm of attendance, the congregation, the physical familiarity of the church, its smell of candles and incense—yes, even the bingo when my wife pushes me into it. I know I'm perpetuating something staid and prosaic, but I feel good in it. I guess the bottom line is that I don't want to be a loner—to map my own spiritual life. I need to belong."

"But you can do both," I suggested. "Stay in your church and explore universal spirituality at the same time."

"But if I dabble outside my religion, I'll lose my friends. You know how some people are—'You're either with us, or. . . .' "

"I know," I said. "I've got the same problem. But shouldn't we be willing to pay some price for what we want? Look at the price Jesus' disciples paid for a great idea. They cut themselves off from their families."

"But I'm not as smitten with your idea as they were with Jesus. I might add, to inject universalism into organized religion is like using a shovel to move the Himalayas."

"That's what the Romans must have said to the early Christians."

"I don't buy that analogy."

"Why not?"

"Because Jesus glorified God in a way that gripped the hearts and minds of people. Universalism is too impersonal—it doesn't have that miraculous grip. And look: if it doesn't appeal to *me*, and *I* fully understand what you're talking about, how do you expect it to appeal to the less educated?"

"But what Jesus preached was pure spiritual universalism. Unfortunately, it was codified into hard-nosed religion. But just as religious doctrine finally changed barbarian psyches, so eventually spiritual universalism will transmute religious doctrine into spiritual essence."

"George, I understand your arguments, and I admire your optimism, but you're betting on a long shot."

My friend is right.

It *is* a long shot.

But evolution is in no hurry. It will have its way. The universal blueprint is ready, and once the foundation is in, the spiritual edifice will be built.

But it will take many heavenquakes, high on the spiritual Richter scale, before posterity will be blessed with the result.

THE SUPER RICH DISTORT HUMANISM

The super rich work themselves to a frazzle to make their fortunes, then plunge into a whirlpool of noisy living. They buzz over their possessions, fly from one posh resort to another, and surfeit their voracious appetites with pleasure. Rarely do they taste the honey of wisdom.

"George," one of my super rich friends told me, "You could have been in my class if you hadn't fiddled with your spiritual nonsense but instead stuck to making big real estate deals. Instead of your few piddling millions, you could have been a partner in my corporate empire."

Indeed, I could have. John's sales are now $200 million a year, with a net profit after taxes of $10 million.

But I would have had to be doing what he's doing—flying around the country, elbowing into deals in one city, bulldozing competition in another—constantly enmeshed in the turbulence of frenzied activity.

He likes it.

I don't.

He's building layer upon layer of success—I'm flirting with ideas.

He breakdances—I waltz. There's more money in break-dancing, but there's more beauty in waltzing.

John is a razor-sharp humanist, a social and charitable pillar of our community, and by many standards a fine man. But the most important ingredient for a holistically fulfilled life is lacking—spiritual wisdom.

Not that he couldn't acquire it; but he's too harried and hurried to look for it.

That's why wealth and wisdom seldom mix.

Gene was another one of my super rich friends.

I had made several deals with him when we were getting started, and we had kept in touch while he was racing ahead of me. His X-ray business vision had catapulted him into a $100 million fortune.

But Gene had a problem.

He was depressed.

"I'm on a projectile, hurtling into bigger and bigger deals," he told me one day, "and I don't know how to get off—or whether I even should. I'm smart enough to know that piling up more money doesn't make sense anymore, but what can I do? I have no hobbies, and I wouldn't know what to do with myself if I stopped. And I'm *afraid* to stop! You've been writing about how to find something big to live for. Have you got something big for *me*?"

"Begin to decompress," I said. "Work selectively on projects that make a contribution to society, and start reading some of the classics that I'm sure you've always wanted to read but didn't have time for. That'll slow you down enough so you can get off your projectile."

"Good advice," he agreed, "but so difficult to follow. You see, George, it was so hard to make a buck when we were getting started, but now that I know where, with whom, and how to make millions, it's so tempting and so exciting to go on and on. I've tried to read serious things—the Bible, for instance—but within minutes my mind wanders off into some juicy deal.''

"What if someone offered you a year's contract to pick up and keep $100 bills, with the proviso that you had to do it eight hours a day, 365 days a year? I'm being facetious, of course, but would you agree to it? Of course not. But in a way, you're doing the same thing, except I suppose it's more interesting making deals than scooping up $100 bills. If you look at it that way, perhaps you'll take a break from scooping up millions and turn to an interest, like exploring reincarnation, or how the wisdom of the East differs from the wisdom of the West.''

"I guess I'm too deep into my thing. What you're talking about doesn't get the slightest rise out of me," he said with a sigh.

A month later the papers announced that Gene had become involved in a $50 million shopping center deal. The classics, reincarnation, the wisdom of East and West were no match for his consuming interest in pyramiding wealth.

The Bible is right: wealth often blocks out wisdom.

PART VI

How Human Dry Rot Spreads in a Spiritless Vacuum

When there's nothing to hold onto except human reason, it's easy to slip into warped rationalizations. Without a spiritual base from which to develop moral standards, desires run amuck.

Each of the following four profiles is the story of an individual falling prey to the siren calls of aimless ambition or purposeless pleasure—the weaknesses of wheeler-dealers who unwittingly lead noisy, rudderless lives.

CHAPTER 17

How Raw Ambition Collapsed a Real Estate Empire

Sid was regarded by knowledgeable people in his field as one of the most creative real estate developers America had ever produced. He built and managed office buildings, shopping centers, apartment complexes, and hotels in New York, Chicago, Denver, and Washington, D.C. His advice on how to revitalize our country's downtowns was in great demand.

The realtors in Milwaukee had invited him to speak on upgrading our downtown, and I was chosen to introduce him to a prestigious real estate audience. He was at the height of his career and estimated to have a net worth of $100 million dollars.

He agreed to see me in his hotel room after his talk to the realtors.

"You started with nothing," I began, after I was comfortably seated in his plush suite, "yet in a short time you rose to the top. How did you do it?"

"America was ready for a new take-off, a burst of enterprise. It needed men like me with three go-getting prerequisites—guts, imagination, and persuasion. One or two are not enough. It has to be all three. And I've got 'em all. That's why I am where I am."

"What about a fourth?" I ventured. I had heard about his bulldozing reputation.

"What fourth?"

"Integrity."

"Success manufactures its own integrity. Business people are impressed with results, not integrity."

"How did you get your results?"

"Results are based on sound theory," he said, striking a professional pose. "Before you get refrigerators, you have to know the laws of refrigeration. Before you conceive a multi-million dollar development, you have to know the law of supply and demand; the characteristics of a particular city; where financing is available; and a dozen other specifics. After you determine them, you rev up your guts, fire up your imagination, and go for the jugular with aggressive persuasion—the three requirements I mentioned."

"What do you mean—*jugular*?"

"Going in for the kill. For instance, when I became convinced that one of our largest cities needed a new $15 million office building, I overwhelmed the mortgage people with a flurry of statistics that justified a $15 million value and a $12 million loan. Of course, I knew I could built it for $12 million and therefore could get into the deal with my elbows."

"You mean with no money of your own? Didn't the money lenders know what you knew?"

"No. If they did, they'd be doing what I was doing."

"Well, how did you build the $15 million building for $12 million?"

"I cut the hell out of contractors' prices, I gave the interest-loving moneylenders an extra half-point interest to make them pant for the excessive loan, and I cut construction time from eighteen months to one year."

"How did you do that?"

"Work three shifts."

"Didn't the people who lived nearby complain about the noise at night?"

"Sure, and they threw a lawsuit at me. So I hired a smart local lawyer who stalled the case until I was finished."

"Didn't you make a lot of enemies—a New Yorker disrupting their city?"

"Yeah, but I got results. My New York mortgage bankers were more interested in results than in how I got 'em."

"Do you sell any of your projects?"

"Hell, no! Why should I sell and pay income taxes? I can build all the buildings I want without any of my own money."

"Have you any hobbies?"

"None; I'm too busy."

"Any other interests than making money?"

"Are you insinuating there's something wrong with making money? If you are, remember: I'm creating wealth and jobs. That's more important than writing books or painting pictures. I meet people's needs; artists only concoct illusions."

"Apparently you have no use for art; but how about religion? Does God play a role in your life?"

"I was told I'd be introduced by a hard-hitting developer—so what's all this about religion . . . God . . . ?"

"Why can't one be a hard-hitting developer and a fervent believer in God as well?"

"I'll be blunt. God is something people have concocted to give them security. I've *got* security. God is for weaklings, not for gutsy guys."

"I gather you have a master plan for each project. Do you have a master plan for your life?"

"Like what?"

"Like linking your business genius to something bigger?"

"Like what?" he again asked brusquely.

"Like releasing the grip on the jugular and beginning to care for people as much as for profit."

"You're a strange bird. What's with you?"

I decided to hit him hard, just to get his reaction.

"Would it shock you if I said that God is chairman of the board of my business enterprise?"

"You're not only strange; you're an oddball, an impractical dreamer."

"Not as odd and impractical as you think," I said, getting my dander up. "Let me offer a few observations. Without a spiritual overview, genius is easily distorted and corrupted. Haven't world-famous artists ruined their lives with selfishness and dissipation? And couldn't businessmen, blinded by profit, also lose their marbles?"

"What are you trying to say?"

"I see several dangers in holding onto all your highly leveraged real estate—and you're shortsighted about not wanting to pay income taxes."

He perked up. I was now talking his language.

"Give me reasons for your opinions. They strike me as amateurish."

"Fixed expenses, as you and I know, are generally 50 percent of gross rent. And if the interest and principal on your highly mortgaged properties are about 40 percent, then, when you run into a cyclical recession as we surely will, and your occupancy drops to 80 percent, you can have a 10 percent negative cash flow and drown in a sea of red ink. Holding on to your real estate because of your unwillingness to pay income taxes could boomerang."

"How?"

"By not selling some of your properties, you could deprive yourself of cash you may need to see yourself through a recession."

A recession did in fact hit Sid, and his negative cash flow was so immense that his properties began to topple into foreclosure one after another.

Even though Sid was floundering financially, the leading developers of America paid tribute to his genius by inviting him to be one of the panelists in a symposium on the future of commercial real estate.

The president of one of the largest real estate organizations of America, a good friend of mine, was chosen to introduce Sid to several hundred leading developers of our country. Two years earlier Sid had cheated him out of a $250,000 commission. But my friend's wisdom generated enough generosity to block out Sid's wrong and concentrate on Sid's pioneering contribution to the real estate industry.

"Let's not forget," he told the real estate elite, "that Sid plunged where others feared. He was the lion-hearted genius who taught us the subtleties of sale leaseback, what to look for in regional shopping centers, and how to finance office buildings and hotels in cities where none existed. Let us honor a real estate genius and acknowledge his enormous contributions to our industry. Let us salute a pioneer."

When he finished, the audience spontaneously rose to its feet and gave Sid a thunderous ovation, forgetting for a moment the dark side of his personality with which many were familiar.

Looking contrite and without a trace of his former arrogance, Sid put his arm around my friend's shoulder and, with tears rolling down his cheeks, said:

"I'll never forget what you said as long as I live."

CHAPTER 18

Otto Drank His Life Away

Otto was a star salesman. But he had one main defect: his performance at bars was as stellar as his talent in making deals.

His B.A. in philosophy honed his logic and gift for words. Of all the philosophers he had studied, Otto preferred Epicurus. Using his mentor's rationale, Otto defended his alcoholic addiction with a persuasive flair.

"Y'know," he said, after he had had a few martinis at lunch while we were discussing a real estate deal, "there are five basic philosophies of life. Do you know what they are?"

"I think there are as many philosophies as there are philosophers," I replied.

"That's a superficial notion. No, they all fall into five major categories. The average layman hasn't the faintest idea what they are. I guess you're one of them. Want to know?"

"Go ahead. What are they?"

"Epicureanism—the joy ride. Stoicism—ultimate self-control. Platonism—putting first things first. Aristotelianism—setting your sights high. Love—based on a belief in God. I reject the last four and eagerly embrace the first—the joy ride. Liquor gives it to me—a delightful euphoria that's a pleasure to my senses."

"But your delightful euphoria could ruin you. You've got

so much going for you—intelligence, charm, ability, and a fine family. But to be blunt, I think you're cheapening it all with your drinking."

"I don't mind the word *drinking*, but I resent the word *cheapening*. I don't hurt anyone. Let me quote Epicurus: 'Make pleasure the alpha and omega of life.' That's what I'm doing. And to quote him again: 'A life of pleasure can be practiced with prudence, honor, and justice.' I go along with that too. I practice it."

"Despite what your hero says, I don't think drinking at bars is prudent, honorable, or just. You've put your mind in a noose."

"What you call a noose is a wide world of pleasure. It's there to be enjoyed—to the full. That's Epicurus' way, and mine too."

"You've swallowed the bait of one philosophy, and you're hooked on it. What would happen if, for one reason or another, you should suddenly be cut off from your main source of pleasure? You'd be lost in despair and self-pity, wouldn't you? And by the way, how would you like to live in a society full of epicurean hedonists?"

"I take the world as I find it. If people prefer noble philosophies to make it safe for me to practice mine—why not take advantage of it? I like to mingle with people—that's where deals are. I make most of mine at bars. Of course, that's where I make other deals too—deals you might not approve of!"

"But isn't it a barren philosophy? Don't you find it boring to spend night after night at bars? Besides, what about your wife and children? Is it fair to them? You're fair in business—why not be fair to them? You baffle me."

"While you're being baffled, I'm having the time of my life! I'm a hedonist through and through, and I love it!"

Four years later, Otto walked into my office and closed the door.

"George, I've reached the end of my life. It's over. I've just returned from the doctor, who told me that unless I give up drinking, my days are numbered. I have cirrhosis of the liver. I'm trapped. Without drinking, life would not be worth living. But with drinking, the alternative is just as bad. What do I do?''

Gone was his former flamboyance. His jaundiced face and eyes mirrored defeat. I had to keep from asking, ''What would Epicurus do?''

''So your drinking has finally sprung its trap. But fortunately you can get out of it because you have a built-in healing system, the natural wisdom of your body. Stop abusing it, and your liver will get back to normal. Excessive drinking got you into this; right living can get you out of it.''

''But George, how can I give up drinking when it's number one in my life?''

''Don't be a fool. Remember the story of the prodigal son?''

''I do,'' he said, with a faint smile crossing his pale face. ''But how does it apply to me?''

''You can go back to your family—a new, sober man. By trying to make them happy instead of seeking happiness only for yourself, you boost your chances for a new life.''

''It won't work. In the Bible the prodigal son was eager to go back, and he was warmly received. I'm not eager, and my family is estranged.''

''Apologize for the grief you've caused them and see what happens. It's a first step toward letting God in your life.''

''You know what I think about God—nothing. I'd be embarrassed to mention Him. God has been a stranger in our house all our married life.''

''Why not start with Alcoholics Anonymous? They've kindled God in many spiritless vacuums. Why not in yours?''

''Not me, George. I'm too far bent from what you're talking about.''

''A blacksmith can bend unyielding iron by applying heat. You can be bent to normality by a fiery desire to change. I've seen it happen in more unbendable situations than yours. All you need is the will to change. There's so much at stake!''

''But I don't have the will, and it's too late.''

After a few minutes and a sad goobye, he left.

Several days later I heard that Otto was back at his old haunts, living his epicurean philosophy to the hilt.

Eight months later, he was dead.

Because Otto chose Epicurus to guide him instead of God, he lost his way—and his life.

Unless intelligence is used holistically, instead of being compartmentalized into sheer money-making or pleasure-seeking, we fragmentize our life.

CHAPTER 19

Rhumbaing Became Herb's Obsession

Without a moral standard against which to measure his life, Herb, a retired 63-year-old millionaire, danced away his marriage.

I met him in Jamaica while vacationing in Montego Bay.

Night after night while he rhumba'd with young girls at nightclubs, his 60-year-old wife remained in her hotel, fuming with frustration. The rhumba king, as he was called, swiveled his hips and turned his torso with the grace of a professional dancer.

"It wasn't always like this," his wife told me one morning at the Cove, Montego Bay's world-famous tourist beach, while Herb was sleeping off his nightly rhumbaing.

"He was a poor, ambitious young man when I married him. We were romantically in love, until his business success began infecting our relationship. The more successful he became, the less attention he paid to me and to our children. Oh, we kept up a semblance of respectability by occasionally attending church services, family weddings, and giving to charities. But underneath this veneer of unity, we were both miserable. I criticized him for grandstanding publicly and neglecting us privately. When I disturbed his peace at home, he increased his carousing away from home."

"What did you do about it?" I asked.

"I threatened divorce, but that only widened the gulf between us. I didn't go through with it because I took a realistic look at my alternatives. With him, I kept my family together and had all I had dreamed of when I was poor—a beautiful home, grand vacations, fine clothes, expensive jewelry. Everything except his love. Without him, I would have a divided home and loneliness. I'm not the type to go out looking for men. What I see are not much better than what I have, anyway. So I've decided to adjust and endure. He does his nightly dancing, I do my knitting and reading. So with all our money —we've got nothing!"

A rested Herb came out to the Cove in the afternoon. His wife introduced us. Her lament had piqued my curiosity, and I was interested to find out what kind of man was on the other side of the tarnished coin. After moving to a quiet spot on the beach, I started the conversation.

"I understand you were in the wholesale plumbing business. I'm a real estate developer, so I've had a lot of dealings with the plumbing industry."

"Then you must be rich, because all the developers I dealt with were millionaires."

"I've done well, but I'm more interested in spirituality— it's more challenging."

"What can you do with spirituality in Jamaica? You're in the wrong place!"

"Spiritual interests are for everyone, everywhere."

"Not for me! I'm for fun, for dancing, rhumbaing. It's got spiritual things beat off the map! Have you gone to any of the night spots around Montego? They're great! And the mulattoes—they're the sexiest . . . and what dancers! . . . and what. . . ."

He was coming on strong.

I stopped him.

"What about your wife? How does she feel about all this?"

"What do you mean, my wife? She's all right. I've worked hard, made a lot of money, and all I want now is fun. What else is there if you have the desire, the vigor, and the money? If you don't know, I'll tell you."

"What is it?"

"Doing the rhumba, the calypso, and fooling around with girls. Does that shock you?"

"It does that you should settle for so little. Shouldn't a successful man like you help eliminate some of the chaos in the world, instead of adding to it with your philandering?"

"What's with you? Are you some sort of priest? Don't you know that a woman is the most wonderful creation on earth? And when she dances, she's the most desirable. You don't feel the way I do, so you can't thrill to her flirtatious looks, the subtle sway of her body. A woman is the greatest invention! She started the oldest profession, and it's still around. Does it tell you something? . . . why it's lasted so long?"

"Aren't you idealizing woman and demeaning her at the same time? Isn't breaking your marriage contract with your wife demeaning her? Doesn't that bother you?"

"You're naive! Haven't you used a loophole to break a contract when it was to your advantage? I have. And so did King David when he sent his best friend to battle so that he could have his wife. There's nothing wrong, my friend, with having many women. King Solomon did; religious Mormons do; and the smart Arabs. And so do I. The fact that I'm married is only a cultural technicality. You can have it your way, I'll have it mine."

"Don't the Ten Commandments mean anything to you?"

"They were for Jews 3500 years ago, not for me."

"Have you any children?"

"Two married boys."

"Want them to treat their wives as you do?"

"You mean screwing around—no need being tactful. They already do. The fruit, you know, doesn't fall far from the tree."

"And you're content to have your sons live that way?"

"Why not? Let me tell you something. When you don't

have a strong sex desire, it's easy to be a moralist. It's easiest for a eunuch. I'd rather be a sexual macho than a moralisitc eunuch.''

''But are you satisfied to be macho to your dance partners and a eunuch to your wife?''

''You're not going to confuse me with words. I listen to no one but myself.''

''Ever listen to God?''

He was startled by my question.

''I can't figure you out. What's this with God all of a sudden? Look, I only believe in the here and now. Oh, I go to church occasionally when I have to; but do I believe in God? Can you see Him? Touch Him? People tell themselves that enjoyable things are sinful and get cramped with guilt. Not me. I don't live in heavenly clouds. I live right here on earth, satisfying my five senses—to the hilt. That's real. That's fun. That makes me feel great. Go ahead, you can dream about God. I want to stay awake and enjoy myself.''

''But if successful people don't take responsibility to shore up what's bad in society, it'll collapse and drag you down with it.''

''You're talking about things that may mean a lot to you but nothing to me. You haven't budged me an inch. And you'd be a fool to think you can. I warn you, I'm a very persuasive fellow. I may change *you* before you change *me*. If you're game, come with me tonight, and tomorrow we'll have another discussion. I'll put my earthly evidence against your heavenly dreaming. Then we'll see who makes more sense.''

''I know what's visible, but do you know what's Invisible?''

''Look,'' he said with a grin, ''guys like you would have nothing to shore up if it weren't for guys like me.''

''What does your wife think about all your gallivanting?''

''She doesn't mind it anymore. Or rather, she doesn't care. She's stopped fighting me. Our differences have been resolved in a sprit of resigned peace.''

''You mean marital death?''

"Call it what you will. By the way, you're getting awfully personal. But I don't really mind, because you're an interesting prober. It gives me a chance to ventilate my values and develop a logic to support them. So far, I'm doing all right, don't you think?"

"What would you do if your wife began cheating openly the way you do?"

"I probably wouldn't like it, but I'd get used to it, the way she did."

"You sound like a male nymphomaniac."

"Whatever it is, I'm guilty. But don't sell me short. I'm a college graduate. In one of my literature courses, I had to read *Brothers Karamazov*. The character that fascinated me most was the father of the brothers. He pictured every woman he met in terms of how she would yield to him in bed. I must have a bit of his personality, because I think the same way."

"Have you ever given any thought to the idea that sex with one is more romantic than sex with many? If educated men like you settle for promiscuity instead of romance, then we'll sink into the quagmire of an X-rated society."

"You're ruining my vacation," Herb said.

He got up and left.

Intelligence alone is a thin reed to lean on. Without a grip on spiritual purpose to help us develop our higher human nature, we either remain where we are or drop deeper into our physical senses.

Herb's evolution not only stopped—it dropped.

CHAPTER 20

"I'd Rather Be Smart than Intelligent"

Richard was a real estate tycoon who had pyramided a $50 million fortune. I heard him wisecrack to his college-educated investment portfolio manager: "You're intelligent, but I'm smart. That's why you're working for me and not I for you."

The obvious inference was that astuteness will get you where intelligence won't.

In one of my discussions with Richard, I rated wisdom, intelligence, and smartness in that order of importance.

"Wrong!" he said with bravado. "The intelligent are too scholarly and the wise too cautious. Only the smart go in for the kill and become Number One!"

Using his astute business savvy, Richard had become, by age 60, one of the ten leading real estate moguls in the country.

At lunch one day, I asked: "Are you happy? Fulfilled?"

"Neither. How can you be happy and fulfilled when people are trying to screw you every chance they get?"

"How do you handle them?"

"I screw *them* before they screw *me*! And I'm the evidence. Many of my competitors are either on the ropes or bankrupt."

"Don't be offended, Richard, but what about your lousy reputation? Doesn't that bother you?"

"First off, screw you and the guys who think I have a lousy

reputation! What you and they think doesn't mean a thing to me.''

''I'm sorry if I offended you,'' I retreated; then I added, ''but if you add a little morality to your financial wizardry, you could enjoy both your wealth and a good reputation. Anything wrong with that?''

''George, you're a naive dreamer, spouting wisdom and morality. I'm too smart to waste time babbling about what doesn't count.''

''No one will ever accuse you of not being smart. But is that enough? Unless capitalism gets an infusion of morality, we could end up the way the Romans did.''

''You're getting too serious—and boring. Skip it! Let's talk about deals. I happen to have one you'll like. It's got a lot of subtle ramifications, but if you haven't lost your money-making marbles, you'll grasp them easily. Care to listen?''

''Go ahead.''

''We're presently in a going-public craze. If you still own the Bockl, Prospect, Marshall, and Riverwood Buildings, I can get you $5 million in cash for your equities and still allow you to retain 25-percent interest in a $20 million public real estate offering. This should sound good to you, because if you stood on your head, you couldn't get more than $3 million for your equities, and not in cash either. Based on our previous discussions and my good memory, I would say you owe about $5 million against your properties.''

''What's your plan?''

''I can get your properties appraised for $10 million. That will give you a $5 million equity position—instead of $3 million. I own a prime site of 200 acres outside of Boston that is ripe for a regional shopping center which will appraise for $3 million. I'll throw in several other pieces of real estate to match your $5 million equity so that we'll own the corporation fifty-fifty. We'll then sell 50 percent of the stock to the public for $10 million, and split $5 million apiece between us. Your real estate will provide the bread-and-butter income for our deal, and my shopping-center site for future growth. It'll be a balanced real estate portfolio. And if the corporation takes off, we could make another few million for our 25 percent interest. What do you say?''

His eyes gleamed, and his voice crackled with excitement.

''What if the growth doesn't materialize and the stockholders find that their $10 million is worth only $4 million or less?''

''That's the chance they'll have to take. Nothing is guaranteed.''

''Let's stop and analyze this. You've added $2 million of water to my real estate and, if I read between the lines, $4 million of foam to yours. I don't think it's fair. What if some elderly widow invests $10,000—half of what she owns—and our deal drowns because it's overloaded with foam and water?''

''You're too iffy and too negative. That's not the way to make deals. You've got to be positive.''

''With somebody else's money?''

''Well, George, it looks like you're saying goodbye to $5 million.''

''But holding onto ethics. That's more valuable than being smart.''

''Well, have it your way. You've just ruined a great deal.''

''And maybe prevented a lot of headaches.''

Several years later I learned that Richard headed up a $50 million REIT, an acronym for Real Estate Investment Trust. The stock sold at $20 a share, and several years later the buyers couldn't sell it for $2 a share. Dozens of such trusts were formed in the late 1960s, and almost all of them either went bankrupt, or their stock was sold for a pittance of their original subscribed amount.

Richard's REIT deal was a dramatic demonstration of how the smart get smarter; the rich, richer; and the poor, poorer.

He bought back thousands of shares at $2 of the defunct REIT that he had floated at $20 a share. He kept them for several years until inflation brought the values of real estate up again, then sold his $2 stock for $15 a share. He made millions on both ends of the deal, while the buyers and sellers of the stock lost much of their savings.

I saw Richard again after he floated a successful, financially intricate bond issue.

"You're piddling around with recycling old buildings and renewing run-down neighborhoods," he told me, "when you could be making millions floating stock and bond issues. That's where the money is. Remember how you lost $5 million when you turned down my scheme to go public a few years ago?"

"And I'm not sorry. You and I have different philosophies about business. Mine is to make a profit out of creating wealth —reviving neglected buildings and rejuvenating old neighborhoods. Yours is parasitic—manipulating paper equities. The result: big guns like you win, and popguns who trust you lose. Those in the know devour those who don't know. Isn't that the bottom line of what's happening—the lions devouring the zebras?"

"That's a fancy way of putting it. But let me put it another way. Didn't Darwin propound the theory of the survival of the fittest? Why should I settle for thousands when I can make millions?"

"I'll tell you why. Over the past decades, the ultrasmart lions like you in South and Central America have usurped most of the land and the businesses by outsmarting the zebras. But by doing it, they've mined their land with political and economic explosives. The haves and have-nots, the Fascists and Communists, are now at each other's throats because the Marcoses and Somozas of the world have foolishly chosen to

be smart instead of wise. Their cunning greed and obscene ac-
cumulation of wealth are blowing up in their faces. They've
become victims of the survival-of-the-fittest theory. We can
no longer practice it and survive. We need a new theory—the
survival of the wisest. Unless we begin practicing it, Capitalism could become the dinosaur of economic theories.''

"What do you mean, survival of the wisest? Climbing an
ivory tower where the dilettantes are? Not me! I'm enjoying
what I do. It gives me bounce, excitement. It's a wonderful
game. I'll never give it up for some fuzzy wisdom theory.''

"Don't you prefer gratefulness to hostility?''

"Can you deposit gratefulness in the bank?''

"But how much is life worth if it's polished on the outside
and decaying on the inside?''

"Your highfalutin' philosophy is not for me. Moralists like
you are a dime a dozen, but guys like me—we make things
happen!''

"Let me end with a parable, Richard. Ten thousand years
ago, when killing wild animals was the main source of food, a
hunter got up early in the morning to make his kill. He was
an expert with the bow and arrow and knew where to look.
After several hours he got his prey. Others who were poor
marksmen, or didn't know where to hunt, watched the successful hunter drag his kill to his cave. Game was scarce and
the hungry men who lurked in the woods sent a message asking for a piece of the animal. The hunter refused. 'We're
starving,' the messenger pleaded. Still he refused. A day later
they stormed the cave, killed the hunter, and divided the
quarry. Does this send a message to you?''

"Yes. The hunter should've gotten a few of his sharpshoot-
ing buddies and fought them off!''

"Wouldn't sharing have been the better solution?''

"No. I'm for Ayn Rand's me-first conservatism—looking
out for Number One. That's what Adam Smith proclaimed

two centuries ago, and that's good enough for me. As for your parable, here's your answer: If I'm a top marksman, if I'm willing to get up early in the morning, if I know how to stalk, I don't want those who are lazy and unskilled, who don't know where to look, to force me to share my kill. I'll give only when I choose to give. And to bring your parable up to modern times—I'm against taxation that transfers wealth to the lazy and incompetent. That should give you a pretty good idea what I think of your parable.''

Business is not a game, and winning is not its name. Those who impoverish their victims and drive themselves to coronary brinkmanship may be smart in the short run, but they're fools in the long run.

Without a spiritual compass, they myopically steer themselves and society into future storms.

Part VII

The Spiritual Dynamic of Quiet Time

What is quiet time? It's the shutting off of external thoughts for a while and tuning into the Universal Consciousness, in which our own is rooted. When the mind is quieted, insights come in that normally don't while we're on the run. These insights are God's response to our willingness to listen, and they're invariably of a nobler nature than our ordinary buzzing thoughts.

Quieting the mind prepares it to become a gateway to clear thinking, to feel the rise of spiritual sensation. It's a time when we plant the seed that ultimately produces the fulfilling activity we seek.

CHAPTER 21

A 2000-Year-Old Way of Going to Church

A daily quiet time with God can be more personal than a talk with our closest friend, and more rewarding. It's a new way of going to church that's 2000 years old, the way Jesus did.

When I was introduced to Moral Re-Armament and met dozens of extraordinarily people who used daily quiet time to receive God's guidance, I gave it a lot of serious thought. I was attracted by the results—the remarkable quality of the men and women who were self-disciplined by the insights from their quiet times.

I tried it one morning.

All I heard were chattering thoughts. The experience was new . . . strange. My mind was talking to itself. But after sticking to it for several months, my mind chattered less, listened more, and new insights occasionally flashed across my mindscape. Some were fleeting thoughts which I couldn't recall the next day. To forestall their loss, I decided to write them down as soon as I came out of my quiet time.

Over the years, I have filled 37 one-hundred-page notebooks. They provided the core material for much of this book.

Why is quiet time effective? Because when we still the mind, the new thoughts that come in are the Universal Consciousness' response to our desire to change.

It's easy to shrug this off, especially if we're comfortably grooved in a conditioned pattern of living. But from personal experience and from seeing how hundreds of others have changed, I'm convinced that quiet time is not a fanciful exercise but a clarifying experience.

Murky perspectives and old values change.

New insights form new goals.

The veil is lifted on the part of the Invisible.

Selfish motives come under closer scrutiny during quiet time. The difference between right and wrong is seen with less self-centered bias. It speeds the journey from the lower to the higher human nature.

Quiet time is not some idealistic vision that obscures the needs and the joy of practical living. It's not a dour, humorless discipline, a doctrinal self-righteous injunction to walk the straight and narrow.

Rather, it's a self-disciplined morality that challenges us to measure our human motives against what we hear from God during quiet time. It's on the exciting frontier between the known and Unknown. It's on the tip of spiritual evolution. It leads to a great truth: religious rules do not change human nature as effectively as does self-garnered wisdom.

Perhaps I can best explain what goes on during quiet time with this analogy. When we insert a motor into a tub of clear water, the motor is visible and the water is clear. When we start the motor at slow speed, the water becomes slightly turgid and the motor less visible. If we speed up the motor, the water becomes opaque and the motor disappears from view.

It's the same with a busy mind when the brain is running at full speed. The mind and its thoughts become submerged in froth. Quiet time stops the motor so that we can see more clearly.

I never know beforehand what will come out of my quiet time. My first thought is to decelerate my mental motor, putting it on some soothing image like the ocean, sky, mountain, or forest, to slow it down into a meditative mood.

When I'm confronted with a personal or business problem, I take it to my quiet time and wait for an answer. Sometimes it comes with sudden sureness. At other times, it's blurred and incomplete. At those times I don't try to force an answer. I relax and wait.

Often it comes when I least expect it.

Quiet time is an active dialogue with God. Although I don't hear voices or see visions, I know He is as close to me as my next breath. I don't doubt His presence just because His Universal Energy is invisible. Why should that make it less real? Electricity and the concepts of truth and love are also invisible—yet we can manifest them in personal, tangible ways. Since our invisible consciousness is rooted in God's Invisible Consciousness, it follows that when we tune our awareness and listen, somehow our awareness and God's Awareness are linked.

Isn't it reasonable to believe that it's more creative to commune with God during quiet times than while sitting in a crowded church where we're distracted by people, more preoccupied with what is going on outside than inside?

This is not to demean those who attend church services— they can be more character-building than nonattendance or turning one's back on religion altogether. However, there's a vast difference between the casual discipline of the average churchgoer and the moral self-control of the quiet-time practitioner.

Taking charge of our spiritual development requires more self-command than belonging to a church, just as being an entrepreneur requires more responsibility than working for a salary. In one case, we're in charge; in the other, we follow rules prescribed by others.

Out of the kaleidoscope of new quiet-time insights, I began forming a unified master plan for my life. There's more spiritual substance when a synthesis is hammered out of many options than when you remain attached to one particular doctrine. However, it's more difficult to fit the pieces together than following a prescribed belief.

Some of the changes I've made as a result of quiet times were easy.

Since smoking and drinking were only feeble temptations for me, I was able to cut them out completely. When I attended regional and national real estate conventions, I had no problem in separating myself from the loud, liquored talk and carousing that were always a big part of convention conviviality.

Instead of condemning it, I merely observed the hilarity as (much of it) conditioned mistakes, satisfied with the small aims of noisy living. I had been there. I had made the same mistakes. Quiet time taught me that quiet joy is longer lasting than the fireworks of raucous merriment that flash brilliantly for one moment and fade into darkness the next.

My self-imposed discipline made it easier to do the right thing, even when no one was looking. For instance, several months after I sold a property, my accountant discovered that the buyer's attorney had made an error of $5000 in my favor. I sent a $5000 check to the purchaser and received a glowing letter of appreciation. It was not a great deed, but without looking for ways to raise the quality of my life, I would have waited for the buyer to discover the error himself.

On another occasion, a regular church-attending friend of mine sent a letter to Palm Springs, where I was vacationing, asking me to look at some land for him. I knew he wasn't interested in buying land, and I didn't look for any. When I saw him several months later, I called his attention to the letter.

"You really weren't interested in Palm Springs land, were you? Who're you kidding?"

"Put it in your file, dummy, and save your vacation expenses!" he quipped.

"But I don't need the government's money."

"Okay," he replied; "I was only trying to do you a favor."

The idea was that his letter would be evidence on which I could base deduction of my expenses on the vacation trip.

The chief officer of a bank's trust department entered into a sale and purchase agreement with me on a piece of real estate. A week later he discovered that he had no authority to sell it. In the meantime, I had found a buyer for the property at a $10,000 profit.

"George," he said with a troubled look, "if you insist on closing the deal, as you have a legal right to do, I'll look like an amateur. I'd like you to release me from our contract."

I weighed my $10,000 profit against the uncomfortable squirming of the trust officer.

I took it to my quiet time, where the balance tipped in his favor. It was an opportunity to practice generosity.

To these and similar incidents I added other changes.

I eliminated sarcasm, snide remarks, clever retorts, and know-it-all opinions.

I began to observe more and judge less.

I came to realize that comparing was a subtle form of condemning. The "lesser" was not bad; he or she was simply different from the one perceived as better. It was a more magnanimous way of looking at things.

Envy, pride, self-righteousness, and other character weaknesses received a thoughtful overhauling. I had a better understanding why the Prophets had thundered against them.

By soothing my secular work with practical spiritualization, I was able to close 20,000 real estate transactions over a period of thirty-five years without initiating or defending more than three lawsuits. Quiet time played an important role in minimizing confrontations.

I honed an attitude that turned work into fun. I transmuted daily problems into opportunities and challenges. I looked upon my real estate business as so much grist to be ground into spiritual wisdom.

Others have evolved far beyond my puny grasps for change, but my view of evolution is not to compare myself with others —rather, to progress from where I am to where I want to go.

Spirituality without action is as ineffective as action without spirituality.

Action is grist for growth. It should be the centerpiece of any master plan for living. But what kind of action? For me it's trying something new rather than trailing in the old. There's more evolutionary mileage in originality than in repetition.

Since my expertise lay in real estate, that's where I combined my spirituality with firing-line action.

CHAPTER 22

God's Work with an Assist
from Caesar

THE PROBLEM OF SELLING HOMES TO BLACKS
IN WHITE NEIGHBORHOODS

Quiet time became my haven, my temporary retreat, where
I received answers to vexing problems.

One of these involved selling homes to blacks in white
neighborhoods. Most real estate brokers stayed away from
such sales because of white owners' resistance and the
difficulties of financing black purchases.

In the early 1950s, prejudice was rife and desegregation was
new. Do I get myself involved with white prejudice and black
buyers who are not mortgageable? I asked during my quiet
time. Do I help the blacks and hurt the whites?

I chose the underdog.

I assigned part of my sales force to sell adjoining white-
owned houses to black buyers. I was called a blockbuster. I
cushioned the false accusations with the good feeling that I
was helping blacks to break out of their congested ghetto.

Financing black home sales was as acute a problem as prejudice. Many Savings and Loan Associations in effect redlined
neighborhoods when they demanded large down payments
and excellent credit ratings before making loans to blacks.

157

There were many willing black buyers but too many reluctant lenders.

How to break the impasse?

The answer came one morning—an answer that satisfied the seller, buyer, lender, and my organization. Here's how it worked:

The Bockl Company would buy a $10,000 home or duplex from a white seller, sign an $8500 mortgage to a Savings and Loan, and add my $1500 to pay off the seller in cash.

We would then sell the property to a black family for $12,000, with $500 down, and take a second mortgage of $3000—the difference between the $8500 first mortgage we owed and the $11,500 balance the buyer owed us.

In order to get back the $1500 we put into the deal plus a brokerage commission, we sold the $3000 second mortgage at a discount for $2000, and with the $500 we got in cash from the buyer we got our $1500 plus a brokerage fee of $1000.

With this type of financing, where I became personally liable for millions of dollars in loans, we were able to sell 600 homes to black families who could not otherwise have become homeowners. We stretched out the second mortgage payments over the same 25-year amortization period as the first mortgage, so that the buyer's total payment was little more than rent.

Our plan converted renters into homeowners—a societal stabilizer. As we expected, it didn't work perfectly. Many of these new owners left town, or moved out without notice, leaving us with making the first mortgage payments and, in many cases, wiping out the second-mortgage equities. But approximately 550 of the 600 new homeowners not only made their payments but increased their equities and traded their properties for higher-priced ones as they moved further out into white neighborhoods.

The plan had many beneficent rippling effects. It created

new homeowners, originated safe mortgages for the Savings and Loan industry (they were guaranteed by me personally), sold homes of white owners who wished to move further out, and provided jobs for my salespeople. Although my profit from these 600 sales was less than what I normally earned from one successful building project, I felt good about playing a helpful role in the early stages of desegregation.

To be sure, this pioneering action was sometimes discordant.

But because I felt it was more God's work than Caesar's, I was not ruffled by the opposition.

THE AGONY AND THE ECSTASY OF BUILDING THE FIRST HOUSING PROJECT FOR THE ELDERLY

In 1956 a 70-year-old woman, who had been one of my favorite high school teachers, came to my office and, after a few pleasantries, said:

"George, I know there's more money building for the rich insurance companies than building housing for the elderly. But don't you think that, after working hard all our lives, we deserve housing suited to our retirement needs?"

Somewhat sheepishly, I replied, "To be frank, Mrs. Witte, I've been so busy with my new office building that I haven't given it any thought, but I will now. I vividly remember how you helped me. Perhaps now I can help you."

During my quiet time the next morning, there was a clash of motivations—between Caesar's and God's. Caesar's thoughts dominated at first: There's no money in building for the elderly—that's why no one is doing it. But, God answered quietly: If you truly believe in applying self-generated spirituality to your work, shouldn't you put your building expertise where the need is most urgent? You're worth over $2 million. What's the point of going for $20 million or $200 million? Might not your spiritual interest erode somewhere in those big numbers? You've seen what happens to wheeler-dealer tycoons who drive themselves to insensitivity and smother their decent instincts. Do you want that? Stick to small, unusual projects rather than big ones. You've done the first unusual modern office building—why not the first unusual housing project for the elderly? There's more evolutionary progress in being a pioneer than in repeating what's already been done.

God's advice was more convincing than Caesar's. I listened and obeyed.

I bought a three-acre site overlooking the Milwaukee River in a park-like setting. I drew plans for 94 apartments with special amenities for the elderly that had never been offered before—a large meeting room, a library, a small restaurant for the exclusive use of the golden-agers and their visiting children and grandchildren, a hobby shop, prayer room, shuffleboard courts, and the most desirable amenity of all: an outdoor patio for each apartment. An artist drew a color rendering of a rambling white-brick, two-story colonial structure, showing the patios trimmed with black corrugated iron railings, against a backdrop of lush green trees, and the blue Milwaukee River.

Armed with this effective selling piece and a meticulously structured pro forma statement of income, fixed expenses, and cost of construction, I set out to obtain a $500,000 mortgage. I was turned down by a half-dozen Savings and Loan Associations for two main reasons: elderly people are not good rent risks, and the $75,000 allocated for the special amenities was not income-producing.

The uniqueness of the project fired my interest and kept it burning. I was determined to see it through. During one of my quiet times, the thought came to me that since the project was spiritually conceived, it might have to be spiritually financed. How? Who? One thought triggered another. What about Al, my Catholic-fundamentalist mortgage-banker friend? I called him the same morning.

"Al, I've got a problem that only you can solve. Can I see you?"

"Any time," came the cordial reply.

He listened and smiled as I detailed my concept and then told him about all my turn-downs.

"We mortgage bankers have to protect other people's money when we approve loans," he said. "You were turned down because the lenders weren't sure that older people want to live together. Also, retired tenants have little money, and they're not earners. I'll have to turn you down, George, for the same reasons. Don't blame me. Doing Caesar's work is part of my job."

"How about doing God's work?" My pent-up frustration burst at being turned down by a devout Catholic.

"What do you mean?"

"This is a special project which deserves special risk. It's more than a commercial loan. It's a way of helping the elderly who've worked hard all their lives and now want to spend their remaining years in an affordable, beautiful environment. Look, I'm risking $250,000 in cash against your $500,000 mortgage. My risk is much greater than yours. I can be wiped out, and you could end up owning a $750,000 project for $500,000. So much for Caesar's security. What about the old folk's security?

I could see he was moved.

"George, let me see what I can do. You'll hear from me."

Several weeks later he called and said, "George, you've got the loan. I've gone out of my way, and I want you to do the same to make it a success. It's never been done before, and the eyes of the community will be upon us. We'd better not fail."

Riverwood, the name I chose for the project, was successful from many angles—architecturally, commercially, spiritually. Retired schoolteachers, firemen, secretaries, widows, widowers, and elderly couples left their homes and apartments and flocked to the resort-like environment of Riverwood. The special amenities added a social dimension to their lives.

To make it affordable for low-income retired people, I structured the rent 30 percent below market—$138 for a one-bedroom unit and $152 for a two-bedroom unit.

It was far below the profitability of my office building project. But what a difference in inspirational rewards! When my wife and I joined the tenants occasionally in some of their social activities in the recreation area overlooking the forest-clad Milwaukee River, many would bless us profusely for what we'd done for their lives. Several sent poems expressing their appreciation. We even got several wedding invitations from golden-aged couples whose romances started at Riverwood.

Whenever I needed a change from my busily scheduled real estate office, I would leave for Riverwood to spend a few hours with its happy tenants.

The high inspirational point came when I was invited to Washington to share my experience at a National Conference on Housing for the Elderly. President Eisenhower, one of the speakers, exhorted some 1000 sociologists, urbanologists, and real estate developers to plan innovatively for the elderly —to combine specialized housing with special recreational amenities. Awareness of the need of housing for golden-agers was in its infancy then, and I felt the inner glow of a pioneer.

My quiet time had made an innovator out of me, and its rippling effects spread. I spoke at workshops for elderly housing and shared the building plans with several would-be developers and nonprofit organizations. Similar Riverwoods were built in other cities as a result.

I felt a higher-frequency glow from my Riverwood project than from my office building success. I knew I made the right turn in my career when I chose meeting the needs of people in unusual ways rather than becoming an astute wheeler-dealer who conditions himself to put profit ahead of people.

HOW TWENTY LARGE WELFARE FAMILIES
BECAME OWNERS OF NEW HOMES

Without quiet time, I would not have done it.

Two hundred large families with scant means were living on welfare in rat-infested basements. There was a housing crisis for these poor families, and the public media made it visible with pathetic pictures and heart-rending stories.

I sought guidance for this problem one morning, and, as I listened for a solution, an answer came based on my knowledge of available real estate facts.

The city owned vacant lots of razed properties that could be bought for a nominal amount, and the federal government under Title 35 offered 100-percent financing to families who qualified as underprivileged. I joined the two facts into a plan of action which the *Milwaukee Journal* prominently featured in a lengthy news story.

I suggested that wealthy individuals or corporations buy the unsightly, weed-filled lots from the city and build low-cost four-bedroom houses, which upon completion would be conveyed to the poor families. I concluded the description of my plan with an offer to build twenty of those houses myself.

The story stirred up a great deal of interest, and I was invited to appear on television with an activist priest who had gained national attention in connection with a militant group of protesters known as the Black Panthers. Several black leaders who were also on the program spoke in favor of my idea, but the priest, an "organizer" in the black community (although himself not black), lashed out at me.

"You slippery real estate guys are all alike. You're only interested in feathering your own nests. If we dig deep enough into Bockl's plan, we'd find some trick—more interested in himself than in the poor."

I was stunned. This coming from a priest whom I admired

because he was doing so much good for the black community. I reacted impulsively and unthinkingly.

"What makes you think," I asked, "that you have all the right answers? Could it be that your zealous condemnation may be blindly undermining the efforts of sincere people? Remember, all goodness doesn't reside exclusively in you or in your Black Panthers."

At that point, one of the Black Panthers in the priest's entourage rushed to the speaker's table, shaking his fist at me and shouting, "You'll get this in your face if you talk like that to our Father!"

A black leader sitting next to me probably saved me from being assaulted on live television when he raised his hand and said, "Okay, Tom, let Mr. Bockl continue; maybe something good will come out of this."

The confrontation toned me down, but not enough to prevent me from pursuing my main objective as I beamed my words to the TV audience.

"My plan, as I've described it, is practical, and can take many of these large families out of their miserable, rat-infested basements if corporations or individuals will respond. Let's not be swayed by the negative attitude expressed here tonight. Let's do *what's* right rather than haggle about *who's* right. And to put what I'm trying to do where my mouth is, I'm going on record publicly tonight, as I did in the *Milwaukee Journal*, that I will build twenty four-bedroom houses for twenty poor, needy families."

"He'll never do it, and if he does, it'll be because there'll be a big profit for him!" a Black Panther ranted with raised fist from the back of the room.

The next morning, I took the television experience to my quiet time. It focused on this thought: Don't be discouraged by unfair criticism. What counts is how you'll help people. Concentrate on the beneficial result, not on your anger because of false accusations.

I hired a young man with a Master's degree in real estate and instructed him to buy twenty vacant lots, familiarize himself with the FHA rules of Title 35, hire an architect to draw plans, get contract bids, and visit social agencies and select those poor families who were most desperately in need of housing.

After eighteen months of pioneering work, this man, under my close supervision, conveyed twenty brand-new, four-bedroom houses to twenty needy families with six or more children. The county welfare department, of course, made the mortgage payments on the properties, but the families owned them. Because there was no profit to anyone, and because of the low interest on the mortgages, the payments were only slightly higher than the county was already paying for the families in rent. My helper and I arranged to have a social worker aid the families in maintaining and caring for the homes.

My contribution to this project was the $15,000 I paid to the young man plus my effort in guiding it through completion—small compared to the good it pumped into the community. And there was that heart-quickening reward when I visited the large families in their new homes and saw the happy look in their eyes.

I GIVE HIPPIES A CHANCE FOR A PIECE OF THE ESTABLISHMENT

What were the hippies trying to tell us?

I talked to many of them, and during my quiet time I tried to sift through their complaints.

Many were aimless protesters, but a thinking minority made sense. They found the Establishment cold and callous, driven to succeed without slowing down to help them.

When I bought a vacant 40,000-square-foot auto agency building for conversion into a mini-mall of small shops, the thought flashed through my mind one morning that the project lent itself to giving hippies a chance for a piece of the action—changing protesters into entrepreneurs.

Twenty thousand people lived within a two-mile radius of the former auto agency building. Here, I figured, was the purchasing power necessary for local small business to thrive. This type of recycling had never been done before, and that's why it triggered my interest.

With pioneering optimism, I leased stores to hippies who I knew were financially weak, but with the expectancy that they would grow entrepreneurial muscles. I leased 1000 square feet to a young couple who had been operating a run-down record store under the name of Dirty Jack's Record Shop. They promised to clean up their name to Jack's Record Shop. Within a year, I leased the entire mall to twenty-three merchants, most of them first-time proprietors. The eager young tenants, dressed in "Establishment" clothes, were selling plants, purses, yogurt, art, greeting cards, candy, clothes, antiques, books, ethnic foods, jewelry and a variety of gift items.

The hippies soon discovered that it was easier to protest than to stay in the black!

They were developing a new respect for the Establishment.

A third of the tenants became rent-delinquent after three months. Lack of experience, goofing off, and insufficient capital were the reasons.

Failure breeds meanness. I was accused of poor management, and the young tenants, who had joyfully applauded my efforts when they signed their leases, now tore them up and left. My rent roll dropped from $15,000 to $10,000 a month. The project was in the red.

I wrestled with the mall's plight in my quiet time. My good intentions were dashed—but *were* they? I listened:

Didn't I know that several of Milwaukee's large shopping

centers had a two- to three-year shake-out before they became successful? And while several hippies left with rancorous feelings, didn't others prosper? A young couple selling art prints; Jack's Record Shop; two young women operating a tiny print shop; a black woman selling men's accessories—all made it, and all were happily experiencing their first pride of entrepreneurship. Wasn't I making a contribution in helping beginners get started? What if I *was* losing $2000 a month? Doesn't pioneering entail some sacrifice? Doesn't financial defeat teach a different kind of wisdom?

After several years of financial sputtering, the Prospect Mall became a beehive of activity.

It's still not a great money-maker, but young lives are carving new niches in small businesses.

And an old neighborhood has been rejuvenated.

My success in other ventures paid for the loss in Prospect Mall. The good feeling of doing something different, of changing protesters into entrepreneurs, turned the financial thorns into spiritual roses.

I couldn't have developed this equanimity without quiet time.

HOW A RECYCLING IDEA HELPED RETARDED INFANTS

At a Rotary meeting one day, I heard that ten million men and women, year after year, do some form of voluntary public welfare work worth billions of dollars. This set the tone for my next morning's quiet time.

I would volunteer my services for some worthy cause.

I didn't have to wait long. Such thoughts quickly attract opportunities.

A young couple with degrees in sociology and psychology obtained some federal seed money to care for several retarded infants between the ages of one and five. They were children of husbandless mothers who didn't know how to care for problem infants.

A friend of mine, a professor of sociology, became the couple's advisor.

"George," he said at lunch one day, "I need your help. There's a tremendous unmet need among infants who are wasting away at their homes because their mothers aren't capable of caring for them. Jon and Barbara, two former students of mine, have made a start toward solving this acute problem. They are presently in a dilapidated basement caring for a few infants, but there are many more who need their help. To do a professional job, they need a modest school for fifty infants and twenty-five teachers. I've done some checking. To build a new school would cost a million dollars. There's no public money available for such a school. But I've organized a board of directors with a few socialites who might be able to raise $350,000 from private donations for a Montessori project."

"Where do I come in?"

"I'm putting you on the board to find an old building that will lend itself to recycling into a school for fifty children at a cost of no more than $350,000. You're an expert at it. There's no greater need I know of to which you can put your remodeling expertise than to help these hapless infants and their helpless mothers."

The eloquent plea had a double challenge—to help the helpless, and to test my recycling skill.

I explored a dozen buildings and ruled them out either because of price, location, or inadequate structure. Eventually, my search led to a vacated 20,000-square-foot bowling alley building that was owned by a Savings and Loan Association on a $500,000 foreclosure. For years, the sturdy structure had been gathering dust and taxes, adding loss upon loss. I bought it for the Montessori School for $105,000 with $15,000 down.

The socialites went to work raising the $350,000 while I collaborated with an architect and contractors to fit the school's needs into our limited budget. My conviction that deep inside the heart of man is a yearning to do good was amply illustrated by the dozen subcontractors who cut their profits—or even eliminated them—in order to make their contribution to the worthy project. A year later the money was raised, the school was built, and the facilities were as complete and modern as they were originally planned to be in the new million-dollar building.

When I finished my work, the thrill was greater than from the excitement of a successful commercial project.

At the school dedication, my professor friend summed it up:

"All of you who participated in this noble work will experience a healing therapy, different only in kind from the healing the infants will receive in this beautiful school that volunteerism built."

MEETING THE NEEDS OF PEOPLE
OVER 80

After I successfully met the housing needs of the elderly from age 65 to 75 in my Riverwood Apartments, I got a quiet time thought in the form of a question. If a person is over 80 years old, mobile and healthy enough not to need a nursing home, but too fragile to live alone in a big house or apartment, where should he or she live?

It was a spiritual idea with a potential to bear Caesar's fruit. The potential arose from my purchase of a 200-unit apartment building in Milwaukee overlooking Lake Michigan that was half empty.

No one had ever tried to fill this need, and that gave me the additional impetus to do it. It was risky—financially and managerially.

The uncertainty of it only spurred me on.

I converted three adjoining empty apartments into a charming small restaurant, exclusively for octogenarians and beyond, and began advertising for the elderly tenants. I offered a small apartment, switchboard security, a nurse on the premises, a part-time social director, and three meals a day—all for $350 a month for a single, and $550 for a couple in a larger apartment.

Within one year I leased seventy apartments to widows, widowers, and couples ranging in age from 80 to 100. They came from physicians' recommendations in cases where the extreme elderly had no choice but to live alone; from children's homes where both were uncomfortable; and from nursing homes where they had to live alongside the very sick when all they needed was the minimal care I provided to maintain their independence. Several lonely former wealthy businessmen and socialite women came to live at the Knickerbocker, as it was called, not for the low rental, but because there was no better alternative to meet their desire for safe, independent living.

As I was increasing my advertising to fill the 200 apartments with the very old, a social worker from the Department of Health, Education and Welfare visited the Knickerbocker and, although impressed with what she saw, cautioned, "Don't make the mistake of filling the entire building with seniors. Don't institutionalize them. If you want to prolong their independence, put them in the mainstream with younger people. I'd suggest only one-third of the units for the elderly."

She was a wise woman who knew more than I about the psychological needs of those over eighty. I took her through my Riverwood Apartments, where the average age was between 65 and 75. On the way out she said with a smile, "These are your 'swingers.' They're still in the mainstream, but the ones at the Knickerbocker are 'survivors'—they need youth for companionship."

I took her advice.

In order to provide youthful mainstream companionship for my ''survivors,'' I got another idea during one morning's quiet time. I would lease apartments by the week or month and call the arrangement ''home-away-from-home.''

Within a year, aided by innovative advertising and promotion, the Knickerbocker became a home-away-from-home for short-stay executives, visiting professors, trainees, etc. It was used by local people who were dislodged by fire, husbands who were cooling off after arguments with their wives, and families who either had to wait before getting into houses they had bought or had to get out on a certain date after selling their houses.

The very old now had opportunities to mingle and make friends with the ever-changing, interesting people who, in turn, enjoyed the elderly as much as the elderly enjoyed them. The unusual idea of blending the old with the young created a uniquely compatible combination, and rejuvenated a dying building.

It all began with a spiritually motivated idea and, with an assist from Caesar, the unusual venture realized two goals: it met the needs of people, and did it in a profitable way.

CHAPTER 23

Caesar's Work with an Assist from God

I BUILD THE FIRST MODERN OFFICE BUILDING IN MILWAUKEE

In 1954, I attended a Building Owners and Managers Association convention in Denver. One of the attractions was a tour of that city's most modern office building.

After listening to several lectures on the intricacies of building, leasing, and financing new office buildings, I began toying with the idea of building the first modern, centrally air-conditioned office building in my city.

In subsequent quiet times, my human logic tried to dismiss it as a whimsical idea. My real estate experience had been limited to selling homes. But the challenge persisted with these disturbing thoughts: Was a new office building needed? Could I finance it? Could I lease it? Where should I build it?

Back of these thoughts welled up a wave of confidence. It crested with the exhilarating conviction that the uncertainties were not beyond solution, provided I faced the obstacles with equanimity and diligent effort.

Convinced that a new office building was needed, I bought a two-acre parcel of land for $200,000, two miles from down-

172

town, and spent $25,000 in architectural fees with a 30-year-old architect who had my enthusiasm to do the unusual.

With two obstacles out of the way, I now faced the third hurdle—obtaining a $3 million mortgage. I was turned down with a mixture of benign "What nerve!" looks by a half-dozen banks and insurance companies.

What do I do now? I wondered during one of my quiet times.

Try a local Savings and Loan Association, came the answer.

I chose the largest, Mutual Savings and Loan, and presented my reasons for the viability of a new office building to its 85-year-old president.

"The largest loan we've ever made," he said after a week of trying to get an appointment with him, "was $300,000. Tell me, young man: why should we risk $3,000,000 on an unconventional loan to an untried developer?"

The question triggered all my arguments. With six months of practice, I recited them fluently and then added, "Why don't you meet *my* boldness with *your* boldness: I build the first modern office building, and you make the first unconventional loan."

"I like your spunk," he answered. "Let me think about it."

He was a gutsy, self-made man who must have wanted this audacious loan to be one of his last hurrahs, to show his competitors that he still had a lot of dare left. Also, he was a very shrewd lender. He knew that our city was ripe for a new office building.

However, to protect his association and his reputation, he limited his risk by requiring that I put up all I owned as collateral—$300,000 worth of properties and my $200,000 free-and-clear lot. He wrote a clause into the mortgage that if I failed to lease 50 percent of the space within eight months, I would forfeit my $500,000, and the association would complete the building and become its owner.

When the loan was consummated, the consensus of the rumor-mongers was that I was foolish to risk my entire fortune for a pipe dream—and that the aging president of the association approved the loan out of senility.

I now faced my fourth and last obstacle—leasing 200,000 square feet of office space. After three months of hard work, I had stirred up a lot of interest—but only 10 percent of signed leases.

I had drawn floor plans for 10,000 square feet for General Motors, 7000 for Prudential Life Insurance, 5000 for Mutual of New York, 4000 for Zurich of Switzerland, and others, but they all hesitated, waiting for each other to sign first. They were skeptical of my ability to complete the building in time, if at all, and guarantee their moving-in dates. The crisis bogged down into a log jam of indecision, and my time was running out.

Then a flicker of hope!

The Milwaukee General Motors manager was a kindly man who liked my plans and the unlimited parking but refused to sign because "I can't take the risk of entering into a lease and not being sure of moving in. If you can get my superior to say yes, I'll say yes too."

"Where's your superior?"

"In New York."

"Will you call him for me?"

"No—I'd rather you did it yourself." He didn't want to push his boss, he told me.

Within a week, I was on my way to New York.

In preparation for this all-important visit, I posed this question during one of my quiet times: Do I bristle with confidence to gain the man's confidence, or do I give him the details about the precariousness of my position and hope for his empathy?

The answer was simply to use genuine humility.

"Mr. Robinson," I said, after he graciously invited me to lunch in one of the plush GM dining rooms, "you know why I'm here. What you don't know is that your answer will determine the success of a pioneering project—and possibly the fate of my career."

I then detailed the financial structure of my deal, told him how other large companies were waiting for someone to make the first move, and how he could make or break the project.

"Somewhere in the dim past," I continued, "General Motors may have been in my position, looking for someone to take a chance on them. I now ask you to take a chance on me. Big fish should give little fish a chance to swim. That's what enlightened Capitalism is all about, isn't it?"

He eyed me for a while. Then: "All you have going for you is your sincerity. All else is weak. However, I'm going to say yes, and you'd better not fail, or my superior will ask me why I led with my heart instead of my head. It's not often I use them in that order."

Within days after General Motors signed a lease, I placed a quarter-page ad in the *Milwaukee Journal* with this headline:

HERE ARE THE REASONS
WHY GENERAL MOTORS IS MOVING
TO 2040 WEST WISCONSIN AVENUE

Within a month, Prudential, Mutual of New York, Zurich, and a few others signed leases to move into my building. By the time the eight months were up, I had 75 percent of the unfinished structure leased. My cup was indeed running over.

My office building project became a huge financial success. After the debt service on the $3 million mortgage and all fixed expenses, I was left with a $150,000-a-year cash flow and a potential profit of $1,500,000 in the event I decided to sell.

I was flooded with offers to build in other cities. They were tempting.

I took the proposals to my quiet time.

The answer was a definite no. Hadn't I chosen to do the unusual? And wouldn't building in other cities swallow me in commercialism and clog up my cosmic connection?

The message was quiet and clear. Forgo the big buck! Do the unusual!

I listened and obeyed.

QUIET TIME BUILDS THE MADISON INN

When my wife and I visited our two daughters who were attending the University of Wisconsin in the early 1960s, we had to stay in an old dilapidated hotel, several miles from the campus. It was the best in Madison.

I wondered: Why not build a hotel on the campus? It would be a first, for a glaring, unmet need.

The thought gained life during the quiet time months ahead.

As is often the case, an active thought attracts opportunities. Two of my friends bought a lot on Langdon Street, in the center of the campus fraternity and sorority area. With little money and less experience, they tried to build the hotel I had in mind. But they were stymied by zoning laws and the inability to obtain an $800,000 loan.

"George," one of the partners said at lunch one day, "you seem to be getting impossible loans. We'll make you a one-third partner in our hotel on Langdon Street if you can get a mortgage for $800,000, the total cost of the hundred-room hotel. We only had enough money to buy the land."

"I'm interested," I said. "Let me try."

When I met the secretary of the largest Savings and Loan in Madison to explain our financing needs, he was cool for two reasons: I was asking for a 95-percent loan, and I was from out of town.

"But I'm a graduate of the University of Wisconsin," I said; "and my two daughters are here now—so I'm not exactly a stranger."

When he warmed up a bit, I hit home with my most salient selling point.

"Would you agree that some 95-percent loans, if the ingredients for success are overwhelming, are safer than weak 75-percent loans? We need an $800,000 mortgage. We'll add a free-and-clear $50,000 lot, plus the efforts of three hard-working entrepreneurs that're worth $100,000. I realize it's higher than the customary percentage loan, but look at the ingredients for success: The Wisconsin Center a few blocks away holds weekly seminars for out-of-town scholars; hundreds of students' parents and faculty members' friends visit the campus daily; and other out-of-town visitors would prefer to stay in a new hotel rather than in the old run-down hotel you've got downtown."

After the four of us discussed the loan for another half-hour, the secretary said:

"I'll make the loan, but for only $700,000."

I thanked him, then asked his permission to allow us to get a $100,000 second mortgage, a loan from the general contractor. Some lenders don't like second mortgages behind their first.

"I appreciate your telling me this," he said. "If you can get it, I won't mind."

We got it. The builder in effect put in his profit for the second mortgage.

Getting the zoning changed from residential to commercial was a sticky matter.

"Gentlemen," I addressed the zoning board, "we're not out-of-town hustlers coming in to make a quick buck. We're here to meet a genuine unmet need. The finances are in place by two of your town's respected institutions—your largest Savings and Loan and your largest builder. We hope that their confidence in us and in our project will influence your thinking in favor of a zoning change."

After an hour of discussion and a month of waiting, our request was granted.

The hotel was an instant success. My goal of doing the unusual was realized. Caesar was making headway, with a big assist from God.

STORES IN APARTMENTS—A FIRST IN AMERICA

Historian Arnold Toynbee's theory of challenge and response operates not only in the majestic cycles of civilization, but also in small ways among ordinary men and women.

In 1978 when the energy crisis was at its height, and conservation was the cry of the land, I responded to the challenge with an idea that would indirectly save the country thousands of barrels of oil, revitalize our downtowns, and create something that was never done before.

After I bought a vacant, ten-story, 150,000-square-foot, 70-year-old downtown building and was undecided for several months as to what to do with it, an idea came to me one quiet morning that swept me back into the early twentieth century. That was a time when pharmacists, dry goods merchants, and other owners of small stores lived behind their places of business.

Why not convert my building into stores in apartments—small shops in front and living quarters in the rear—? I had room for about 110 such unique combinations. There was nothing like it in Milwaukee, the Midwest, or anywhere else as far as I knew.

Would it work?

The uncertainty intrigued me.

The relative originality of the idea spurred my pioneering spirit, which in turn honed my persuasiveness to convince the Federal Housing and Urban Development Agency to insure a $3,100,000 remodeling loan. In reluctantly approving the mortgage, the Wisconsin H.U.D. administrator cautioned: "You'd better not fail, or I'll be the laughingstock of the agency."